No One Leaves Unscathed

A Woman in the Marine Corps

Stesha Colby-Lynch

BLUE EAR BOOKS

Published in 2024 by
Blue Ear Books
Seattle, WA
USA

www.blueearbooks.com

© Stesha Colby-Lynch

The right of Stesha Colby-Lynch to be identified as the author of the work has been asserted by her in accordance with the Copyright, Designs, and Patents Act of 1988.

All rights reserved. No part of this publication may be reproduced, stored in a retrieval system, or transmitted in any form or by any means, electronic, mechanical, photocopying, recording, or otherwise, without prior written permission of the publisher.

ISBN: 978-0-9990951-4-0

Credits:

Cover Design:
 Sean Robertson

Book Composition:
 Jennifer Haywood, Blue Ear Books, Seattle, WA

CONTENTS

Prologue: Numb Little Bug 1

Part One: The Daughters

Traitor 7
Everybody Loves You 15
He Didn't Have to Be 23
I'm Okay 35
Half of My Hometown 43
Girl Goin' Nowhere 53

Part Two: One Less Day

Build A Bitch 63
Cinderella Snapped 71
Coastline 79
100 Bad Days 85
Last Laugh 93
Twenty-three 99

Hotel Walls 103

Lady Like 111

Memory Lane 119

Somebody That I Used to Know 123

Ruin My Life 129

King of Anything 137

I Need Never Get Old 143

Shivers 149

Victoria's Secret 155

World Spins Madly On 163

    PART THREE: THE TIMES THEY ARE A-CHANGIN'

Last Love Song 173

Nothing More 181

Shadow 187

In the Stars 193

The Good Ones 201

Mean! 205

Soft Dark Nothing 213

Epilogue: A Safe Place to Land 219

About the Author 229

Prologue

Numb Little Bug

I lay in bed with my eyes open as the morning light crept in through the windows. I was exhausted but could not remember the last time I had slept. The voices in my head were screaming, and I couldn't shut them up. They were so loud I could not think. I had taken another pill hoping it would help me sleep; it did not. I took another hit hoping to make everything quiet; it made the voices louder. I thought I remembered going down to talk to my in-laws the night before. My days were running together, and I could not tell up from down. Was it Saturday or Sunday? Sean would be home on Sunday, and maybe I could sleep then. I sighed and got out of bed. My dogs all jumped up to go outside. I was happy that Augie, the puppy, had not had an accident. He was learning. Standing barefoot in the December grass felt good. I let the cold air fill my lungs and stood there in mild discomfort, happy to be feeling something.

    I wished I still smoked cigarettes. This was good smoking weather. I had run out of pot and was committed to not going down to the main house to get more. I wanted to be sober for the first time in weeks. I took one more deep breath of cold air and called the boys back inside. Hercules, the old mastiff, took his time as he didn't move as fast as he used to. Greyson, the pit bull, had developed a stubborn streak and didn't come in right away. Augie always followed Greyson's lead and also ignored me. I raised my voice and was sterner. That got their attention, and they ran up the porch steps. I went to look for my phone to call Brandy. I needed to hear the voice of another live person.

Brandy and I had stayed close since we were teenagers. We got each other through learning to drive, teenage heartbreak, and college in different states. She was now in Mississippi for her husband's job and had a toddler born the week before the lockdown. I hated that I still hadn't met him face to face. Years ago Brandy and I would daydream about our future husbands, our weddings, our children. We had vowed to raise our children as cousins, and now I was watching her son grow up through a phone screen.

"Hello." A groggy voice broke the silence. I must have misjudged the time.

"I'm sorry, I didn't mean to wake you."

"It's okay, little man is still asleep. What's up?" I could hear rustling and kicked myself, knowing she was getting out of bed. What time was it anyway?

"I just am tired. I haven't slept in days. I just cannot seem to calm the voices."

Brandy sounded concerned. "What has been on your mind?"

I sighed. "The usual. This fucking book. I've been thinking about it for days. The words escape my head when I sit in front of my laptop."

I was spinning in circles, pacing up and down the trailer, thinking about this damn book. I just didn't know how I, Stesha Anne Colby-Lynch, daughter to Stephanie and Paul Moreno, could write a book about my life and military service in a way that would be coherent and helpful to people who had been through the same hell I had. I was completely lost and frustrated and felt I was letting everyone down.

"Have you talked to Sean about it? Or your mom?"

"No, Sean is in Dallas working, and Mom is still mad at me. I don't want to hear the disappointment in her voice."

Sean and I were supposed to have joined the whole family a week before in Florida for a Disney trip. I had lied to them about why we had to cancel at the last minute. We told them we just needed to work on the '77 Skyline camper we had bought in Arkansas, and the project was taking longer than we had hoped. The truth was that we were broke. We had quit our jobs, sold our house in Austin to travel, bought the camper with the idea of renovating it, and taken it to the Appalachians before returning to Texas. But after paying off our debts, buying a new SUV, and the three-month trip, we had no money left over and were stranded in an old trailer on my in-laws' property in northeast Texas. The only money coming in was from Uber, but Sean had to go to Dallas on weekends. We had only the one car, so I had no way to leave or make other money. Neither of us wanted to admit to my family that we had blown through all that money in three months. I didn't even want to admit it to Brandy, so I lied some more.

"I just wish she would understand why we couldn't go. We just have so much to do with the camper. Sean pulled out the walls, and the water damage is worse than we thought. The electrical needs to be updated, but Sean knows how to do all that. Eleven years as an electrician before he went to work in Corrections most definitely helps."

"Is there anything you can do other than work on the book? Is there another task to take your mind off it all?"

"All our belongings are in storage. The only things we have with us are camping gear and some borrowed things from Sean's mom. I've cleaned and organized it all several times this week. The TV only gets two channels, black and white reruns or the news."

"Can you take the boys on a long walk? Didn't you say you're on a hundred acres right now?"

That was true, but there were other houses on the property. I didn't want to disturb anyone. Plus, there was a passel of aggressive wild hogs somewhere on the land.

I sighed again. "Everything I manage to write is just crap." I ran my hands through my hair and felt the grease on my fingers. I could not remember the last time I had showered. Or changed out of my pajamas. "Maybe I should just give up."

"No, you can't give up! Your story is too important. People need to know what happened. Otherwise, how will anything change?"
"I know. I just don't know where to start."
"Why don't you start at the beginning. Tell me about Guy."

PART ONE

The Daughters

CHAPTER 1

Traitor

I would love to have met the man my mama married when she was seventeen. In her stories he always sounded so cool and nerdy, and I feel I would have liked him. His nickname was Crash because, when he was the sailing instructor at a summer camp, he had managed to crash a sailboat into a speedboat. He loved science fiction books and played just about every sport. He played the trumpet and had good grades in school. Guy I. Colby V was my kind of cool, nerdy and athletic, creative and intellectual. But Guy was also a troubled young man who ran away from a traumatic childhood to join the Marine Corps, and when he started dating Mama, he was already a raging alcoholic. By the time my conscious memories begin, he was terrorizing my mother and could not figure out how to keep his penis to himself.

Mama met him through her school friend Vanna. Vanna had met him because her father, a retired Army Air Corps pilot, asked her to drop off some things for a fundraiser at the local recruiting office. Vanna saw a lonely young Marine on recruiting duty, looking bored to tears. Guy was stationed at Pendleton but on temporary recruiting duty near Dallas because his grandfather had died. Vanna told him she was going on a double date, and that her friend's date had backed out. Given the choice of hanging out at his strict Mormon parents' house with ten younger siblings or going on a blind date with a high schooler, he chose the high schooler.

Mama was fifteen, Guy was nineteen. And he wasn't the first

Marine she had dated. I never understood how my uber-strict grandparents thought their fifteen-year-old dating grown Marines was a good idea. But if she hadn't, I wouldn't be here today.

Mama and Guy dated off and on, and she even visited him in California for a week with her mother. They drove up the coast, and there's a memorable story of Guy holding Mama's purse while on a boat in San Francisco and a gay man grabbing his ass. There are also not-so-funny stories of Guy using his sister to break up with Mama at a party, and of Mama finding a letter after they were married from a woman he was seeing, saying they were soulmates. But Mama pushed down her uneasy feeling because she needed to leave Dallas.

Guy's siblings and parents were also red flags. At one point several siblings were in the hospital for "migraines" that were really suicide attempts. Some had problems with drugs; others became teenage parents. The biggest red flag of all was that Guy's mother had to get a day pass from the local mental health hospital to attend their wedding.

When Guy proposed to Mama, in her senior year of high school, she said yes. The wedding was planned for that summer. The Marine Corps had other plans. Guy's unit was going to be in Korea. My grandparents let their seventeen-year-old daughter get married over spring break, as long as she agreed to graduate with her maiden name. So, on March 17, 1984, Stephanie Ann Jumper married Guy Irving Colby V at the base chapel. They spent a week in New Orleans, and I was their honeymoon present. Mama tries to say that she wasn't a "teen mom," because she was already married when she got pregnant with me. I always point out that she was pregnant when she graduated high school, and I was born only a couple of months after she turned eighteen. She and I essentially grew up together.

When Guy got home from Korea, Mama headed to California. She was excited to be living walking distance from the beach. She would dig holes in the sand for her belly so she could sunbathe. But just as she was getting used to the idea of having her first baby in California, Guy got orders to Iwakuni, Japan.

Mama urged him to go ahead without her; she wanted to have her baby in America with her family. That decision was the correct one, because Mama got eclampsia and had to be hospitalized at Carswell Air Force Base in Fort Worth. She had to be induced because she was at risk for a stroke and losing her baby. Mama's Lamaze coach, her childhood best friend Karen, carefully distracted her while the doctors tried to get me to breathe. I was early and the labor had been difficult.

The first time Guy saw me, I was a month old. He had come back to the States to take us back with him to Japan. There's a cute story Mama likes to tell about that first night. She got up in the middle of the night and found him staring at me over the crib, just watching me breathe. He just couldn't believe that I was here and was his. At three months, not knowing what to do with an infant daughter, he read to me from *The Hobbit*.

The stories Mama tells about living in Japan in the 1980s are fascinating and poignant. She was unable to work a traditional job because she didn't speak Japanese, and on-base jobs were reserved for spouses whose Marine would be there for a three-year tour. We were there on a two-year tour that was technically "unaccompanied." But in 1985 it was mostly manageable to live in Japan on one salary, so Mama volunteered with the Navy Relief Society and hung out with me. Guy was an advanced swim instructor and was given a summer "B" billet as the lifeguard at one of the base pools. I learned to swim nearly before I could walk, and to read before I was two.

We lived in town since base housing was only for accompanied Marines, so all our neighbors were Japanese. Next door was a restaurant and Mama made friends with the owner, despite the language barrier. About once a week he would knock on the door and ask,

"Baby?" and Mama would hand me over. He would bring me back half an hour later full of chocolate ice cream. Learning to speak English surrounded by people who spoke Japanese gave me an ear for language. Mama tells of Japanese women cooing over my dark curls, and how I understood what they were saying based on my ear-to-ear grins. *Kah-wa-ee-nae* means cute or adorable.

Living on the other side of the world from the rest of your family is isolating enough. Imagine doing it at nineteen and before cell phones and social media. Mama and Guy didn't have a phone or a TV, and they relied on letters that took two weeks to cross the globe. I learned to walk and talk, and Mama couldn't just call her mother or sister or best friend to share the news. She would ride her bike to her friend's house on base. One day Shannon opened the door in tears, and Mama thought something was wrong with the babies. It was January 28, 1986, and the *Challenger* had exploded.

Japan is also where the terror of Guy's drinking and womanizing took hold. Mama told me about Guy thinking she was asleep in the backseat of the car, while he regaled his buddy with tales of all the great prostitutes he had slept with in Korea. Another time Guy was so drunk he passed out cold on the gravel driveway, and Mama just left him there. Mama had trouble stretching their limited budget. One of the worst examples of his neglect was days before payday, when they had just enough for some diapers and formula. She sent him to the store, and he came back with beer and snuff. When Mama went off on him, he told her, "You can ask a neighbor for diapers and formula; I can't ask a neighbor for beer."

On base they were on the "do not accept checks" list. Mama would painstakingly list all their bills to stretch their measly check as far as possible. She could not figure out why the checks would bounce. They did not have a credit card, and debit cards and ATMs had not yet made it to their corner of the world. Guy would receive mail call and Mama would ask him for the bank statements. He said they never arrived. Mama would go to Navy Federal and ask and be told they had been sent. Finally, she asked the bank to send the statements to the branch and she would pick them up. She discovered Guy was withdrawing hundreds of dollars in cash every payday. When we moved, she found the bank statements and bills behind boxes at the top of the closet.

There were also devastating things my mother would have liked to share with her family. On my first birthday she lost her second baby and had to have a D&C without pain medications. The next day she went home, and her husband demanded sex. Only a week later, I was hospitalized with croup and spent Christmas in the hospital.

That's when I would have left. Mama probably would have left too, except she had nowhere to go.

"I can barely imagine how that would be," I said to Brandy. "It is so easy to keep up with each other on social media these days that I forget there was a time without it."

"Same. When my dad was in Afghanistan, we kept up with him on Facebook."

We had been on the phone for over an hour at this point, and I could hear her son crying in the background. "Hold on, little man is finally up. I will call you back after I change him." I took the time to feed the boys and waited on her call.

I wish I could say that life got better when we transferred to Oregon. My earliest memories begin when we lived outside Portland, but few of them are happy. Guy's alcoholism got worse, and he became violent. I clearly remember broken toys; Guy threw them at Mama. I remember accidentally putting too much salt in my macaroni and cheese and being forced to eat it until I threw up. I was three. I also remember being whipped so hard I could not sit down, because I

let my baby sister eat cat litter. Guy had left Karen in my care while Mama was at work. I was four.

There were good moments, though. Mama took us to visit her cousin in Seattle and we explored the Columbia River. She took us to Willamette Falls and Mount Hood. One time I wanted to feed Karen, so Mama propped us up with a pillow on the couch, then went to the kitchen to prepare a bottle. A few seconds later she heard, "Mommy."

"I'll be right there, Stesha."

"Mommy" – this time a little higher pitched.

"Stesha, I'm almost done."

"Mommy!" This time it was panicky.

Mama came around the corner of the couch to see that Karen had rolled off my lap. I had quick reflexes and had caught her by one arm and one leg. I was bent over, holding on to my baby sister hovering a few inches from the ground.

Mama had read a book that said not to lie to your children about big things, so when I asked how my baby sister got out of my Mama, she told me. A few days later, in line at the grocery store, a man told me I had a very pretty baby sister. I responded, "Uh-huh. And she came out of my Mama right here," while pointing between my legs. Mama learned never to tell a preschooler something you don't want repeated in the line at Safeway.

Oregon was a turning point for Mama, realizing that her husband was never going to stop fucking other women. He was on I&I duty, on active duty but working with reservists. There was a young woman Mama suspected was sleeping with Guy. They both had orders to Okinawa, but Guy told Mama that Kristy was going to Tokyo and that his orders were unaccompanied. Turns out they were going to the same place. She found this out from Kristy's mother, who did not realize her daughter was sleeping with a married father of two. I like to imagine that that's when Mama made the decision to leave him. The drive home was a silent one, and the moment she got home she laid into Guy so loud the entire complex probably heard.

Guy was doing everything he could to persuade her to stay in Oregon. After that fight Mama made clear she was going back to Texas and threatened a divorce. Guy laughed and said she would never. I was going to be starting kindergarten in the fall, and Mama wanted me to go to school where she had, in Grand Prairie. I would like to say that her leaving her first husband for her own safety and that of her children meant that life got better. I would like to say the rest of my childhood was happy and safe. Instead, moving back to Texas meant that I was now within the sights of the Colby family.

CHAPTER 2

Everybody Loves You

Leaving Guy was one of the most difficult decisions my twenty-three-year-old mother had ever had to make. She had been raised in the South by religiously strict parents: Divorce was a shameful thing to discuss, much less do. She knew she would have no support from her parents, and that her limited education and job experience would make things difficult.

They had planned a family road trip from Oregon down the coast to Disneyland, then to Carlsbad Caverns en route to Texas. My mother never let on that she really was going to be filing for divorce. The whole trip had been planned and, true to form, Mama sent an itinerary to the family. But when the check the Marine Corps gives a family for moving expenses didn't get deposited as they had expected, they decided to skip San Francisco and go straight to Disneyland. I was almost five and remember squealing in delight on the teacups and hugging Minnie and Mickey Mouse while my baby sister screamed. Then we headed to Arizona to spend a few days with an old Marine buddy and his family. On October 19, 1989, we were watching the World Series between the Giants and the A's in Jim's living room when the Loma Prieta earthquake hit San Francisco. We were supposed to be sightseeing in San Francisco on that day.

We got to Texas and settled in. Just before Guy left for Japan, Mama found a copy of his orders and realized he had turned down accompanied orders and lied about it. A huge fight ensued, and she told him again that she wanted a divorce. A few days later he left, and Mama wouldn't answer his letters and refused his collect calls. He was so furious he ripped the phone off the wall of his shop and threw it across the bay. Since he was drunk at work, he was sent to Phase 6 training, the Marine Corps version of rehab, then home on Humanitarian Leave to take care of his divorce.

On his first night home, Mama let him sleep in the bedroom while she took the couch. She woke up when she felt his breath on her face and screamed when she opened her eyes. She was terrified he was going to kill her and kicked him out. He got an apartment, and Mama would let us go there for a few hours. After one of these visits, I was sitting in the front seat of the car and looked at her and told her she was a "fucking bitch." Out of instinct Mama slapped my face, and I cried. That was the one and only time she ever raised a hand to me. In horror, she apologized and asked why I had called her that. "Daddy told me to tell you that," I told her.

We got back to our apartment, and she called him. "How dare you tell our child to say that. Don't you ever fucking do that again." She hung up on him.

He immediately called back. "I'm suing you for custody."

"Fine! I'm bringing them now. Give me ten minutes." She hung up again.

He called back. "No, I have to work tonight."

"I have to work, too. If you want them, you can have them." She hung up.

He called back. "No, I mean I'm suing you in the future."

"Either you want them, or you don't. You can't have it both ways." She hung up again. She had called his bluff.

He insisted that he would take care of the divorce and told Mama the lawyer required $600 to process it. She didn't have the money but gladly scraped it together and handed over a check. Mama would ask when the court date would happen, and Guy would tell her he was waiting on the lawyer. After months of asking and waiting, she called the lawyer herself. He informed her that the $600 was only a deposit, and that he required another $600 before they would go to court. She called Guy's commanding officer to let him know he had a Marine who was on Humanitarian Leave under false pretenses. Guy was given forty-eight hours to return to Japan. He was livid, but Mama let him come over to say goodbye.

It wasn't until the sheriff knocked on the door to inform her that her checks were bouncing that she realized what he had done. A merchant had filed a complaint, and there was a warrant out for her arrest. Mama was adamant there was a mistake, and the sheriff gave her twenty-four hours to talk to the bank. The bank told her all the checks had bounced because she had withdrawn six hundred dollars. She was floored, reached for her wallet, and saw that her ATM card was missing. The withdrawal was from an ATM on Okinawa.

It was at the end of the summer of 1990 that Guy returned to Japan, and he left active duty that November. After ten years of service, he was not allowed to reenlist, even though Operation Desert Shield had started in August and the Marine Corps doesn't usually let people out during a period of conflict. Guy returned to Texas, drank like a fish, couldn't hold down a job, and mooched off family members. He insisted on being part of our lives, so every other weekend Mama packed us up to go to his place. And by his place, I mean one of his siblings' houses, since he rarely had his own apartment. Surprise, no one wants to rent to an unemployed alcoholic who destroys property. In his mind, the reason they weren't renting to him was that he was a Marine and they were hippies and anti-American.

Occasionally he would be at his sister Melinda's house. Her children Richard and Kayla were only one and two years older than me. Richard and I would get in trouble for staying up all night giggling and talking on walkie-talkies. Other times Guy would be at his sister Patience's, and that was less fun. Patience was nice but had a whole pack of loud children. Plus, her boyfriend was Guy's drinking buddy. They never laid hands on us, but they would scream drunkenly at the TV when their team lost. If we were too loud, they would yell at us for interrupting the game. And there was never enough food to go around. I remember being hungry and sneaking a piece of bread. There was no meat, so I thought I would just put some mustard on it. I accidentally put too much, and Guy caught me trying to throw it away. He forced me to eat the mustard-soaked bread, then ridiculed me when I threw up. To this day I can't eat yellow mustard without wanting to vomit.

Through it all, my mother made sure we had a relationship with the Colbys. She let them take us to church, let them babysit, trusted them. She did not want to punish the Colbys for Guy's actions. She never attempted to sway us to her side, and she never used us as pawns. Mama didn't have to tell us that Guy was a toxic jerk. The problem was that I constantly forgave him. Even though I knew life was easier when he wasn't around, I still missed my father.

"Holy shit! I had absolutely no idea!" I could feel Brandy's anger through the phone. She had been giving little man a snack, and her anger jolted me back to the present. It was now mid-morning, and the dawn mist had evaporated into a sunny winter day. I was still in my pajamas but had put on sandals and was in the yard watching the boys play. Greyson had taught Augie how to wrestle, and they were chasing each other. Hercules was sunbathing not far from where I was standing. I kicked a chunk of grass to the side.

"Yeah, some of this I had no idea about until I sat down with Mama to start writing our story. As I said, Mama never let us know the stuff that went on in the background. I do remember him kidnapping us, though."

Our daycare was told not to let us go home with anyone except Mama and her brother Sam. But they let us go home with Guy, and he took us to his friend's house in the country. The house was the biggest I had ever seen, one of those two-story square farmhouses with a wraparound porch. It also had a stock pond, so Guy wanted to teach me to fish. Each time I asked to call Mama, he gave a reason we couldn't. As the weekend went on I became more and more anxious, and he became drunk and frustrated. He kept trying to teach me how to cast, but my interest was in the plants on the water's edge. Finally, I tried casting and accidentally caught Guy's cheek with the hook. He responded by breaking my pole and throwing it in the pond.

Mama had been frantic, and no one would tell her where we were. The police wouldn't help because "The children are with their father." She screamed herself hoarse until Guy's brother Christopher realized he did not have permission to have us and told her where we were. She called and demanded we be returned. Guy acted like it was no big deal and told her he deserved to take his children fishing.

Shortly after that incident, Guy moved back into his parents' house. About half of the eleven children were still at home, and the youngest, Baren, was only five years older than me. My mother thought it might be good for us to spend time with our grandparents and young aunts and uncles. She did not know why I would bawl on days we went there. She did not know why I would beg to stay home or sleep over at a friend's house instead. When I was eight

I confessed to her that Baren had been raping me every visit for the last two years.

He would hide in the shower and ambush me when I went to the bathroom. He would call me behind the shed and play show and tell while other children played nearby. On really bad nights I can still feel his body on mine, his hand over my mouth. I could hear family members in the hallway and would be frozen in fear. I would hide in closets and close my eyes and pretend I was Lucy Pevensie. But I would have to come out again, and he would find me and tell me that no one would believe me, and that it was my fault my parents were getting a divorce. I believed his lies and told on him only because he made me watch him abusing my baby sister. Even now I cannot stand in a bathroom with a closed shower curtain.

True to form, Mama packed us up and drove to the Colbys' to demand they do something. "Something" was Guy throwing his youngest brother into a wall, kicking in a door, and running away. We didn't see him again for years. He abandoned us when we needed him the most. Mr. and Mrs. Colby asked Mama to speak to their church bishop instead of to the police. She did, because she was certain the counselor would report it to the police, so she didn't have to be the bad guy. Each adult she spoke to urged her to pray about it. Each time my mother would think, "Surely this person is bound by law to report this heinous abuse." When she realized that no one was going to help, she made the gut-wrenching decision to call the police herself. Baren was arrested that day at his middle school, and my sister and I had to go to Cook Children's for examinations. I remember the pain in the doctor's eyes, and that the nurse and my Mama cried.

But courts don't know what to do with a thirteen-year-old sexual predator, so Baren was turned back over to his parents and given counseling. Mr. and Mrs. Colby begged to see us, and my mother made them promise that Baren would not be there. But when Mama pulled up, he would be sitting in the tree overlooking the driveway. She left us in the car while she gave her in-laws an earful, and they defended their actions: "He is our son. What would people say if he weren't here?"

Turns out they knew their son was a pedophile, because of certain "misunderstandings" with other children in their ward (the Mormon word for church or parish), and they did not protect their grandchildren because of how it would appear. He went on to abuse at least three more victims, the youngest his own infant daughter, and each time his parents covered it up and terrorized the victims. There are an unknown number of victims from when he went on his mission in South America. They gaslighted his nineteen-year-old first wife by telling her, "Guy's ex-wife is mentally unstable and makes up disgusting lies." She believed them but filed for divorce when he was arrested for assaulting their daughter. As I write this, he's alive and well and remarried, raising their children because, according to the State of Idaho, he hasn't been arrested enough times to constitute a pattern of abuse. I will never go to Idaho, except to dance and spit on his grave.

Eventually my hard-charging mother made the choice not to involve her in-laws except at our house, and even then rarely. I keep calling Mr. and Mrs. Colby her in-laws, because they still were. Apparently when your estranged husband runs away without a forwarding address, it makes it hard to get a divorce.

CHAPTER 3

HE DIDN'T HAVE TO BE

I heard a sob on the line and wanted to throw up. For several minutes no words were spoken, as we both cried. It had been years since I had said any of this out loud, and my hands were shaking. The baby broke the silence. He wanted a toy that had fallen on the ground. I asked how much he was talking. He would be two in a few months, and it was still mostly baby babble. I asked if I could call back in a few minutes. I stood in the living room and screamed at the top of my lungs. Greyson lifted his head. I wiped my tears and took a shot of whiskey. When my hands stopped shaking, I called Brandy back.

While life undoubtedly was hard for us in those years, there was joy and happiness. Mama did everything she could so Karen and I wouldn't know we were poor. She found us bunk beds and made a slumber party of it, so we could share a room. She had to stretch every penny to afford a two-bedroom apartment. Thankfully, I was a strong and healthy kid. I had bad teeth but good health. Mama likes to laugh about my first sinus infection, when I was in ninth grade. I called her bawling, begging her to come get me from school. I thought my brains were leaking because my snot was green. Karen was sick quite a bit. Her elbows would dislocate with the slightest pressure. Once at daycare it happened while she was sharing a toy with a little boy, and no one noticed for hours. Mama had to take her to the ER, because she didn't have the stomach to pop her elbow back in place herself.

I was the tomboy, always running headfirst into danger and trouble. Karen was the girly-girl who preferred dolls and staying inside. Mama had to bribe me to play Barbies with my little sister for a few hours here and there. The Bailey family lived catty corner from us. Their youngest sons were my age, and we were inseparable through all of elementary and middle school. We played war in the woods and baseball in the streets and fished all summer. I fell out of trees, crashed my bike, got bloody noses from baseballs, was constantly itchy in the summer. I never broke a bone or needed stitches. I was always lucky enough to get up and dust myself off. Karen rarely got hurt, but when she did it was epic.

Once she stepped on a tree branch that had decayed. She landed on her back on a fire ant bed and, by the time the Bailey boys and I climbed down to her, she was screaming. Mr. Bailey heard the bloodcurdling screams and came running and rushed her inside. Mrs. Bailey stripped her down in the shower to get the ants off her. She was covered in painful bites. Karen would trip over her shoes and land, face first, into something sharp. One time was at the bowling alley, and Mama asked her cousin to watch me while she took Karen to the ER. After each ER visit Mama would rob Peter to pay Paul, as she would say. But even then, I remember that first apartment outside Dallas where sometimes the water or power would be off for several days. And we never had a phone. We made do, and Mama did the absolute best she could, hustling and scraping together every penny to keep the creditors at bay.

This was 1991, and she would go into the unemployment office every morning before her minimum-wage job. The new jobs were posted in a large book in the front, and the counselors knew her by name. She wanted a better life for us, where a dinner out wasn't the 39-cent menu at Taco Bell and sharing one soda. She had almost no help from her parents because, to them, divorce was a sin. She couldn't count on her estranged husband's family anymore. Luckily, she could count on her brother and sister for cheap childcare while she worked. I have fond memories of playing under the desk late at night at my uncle's nineties-era computer business, while he and his partner plucked away on those giant Apple computers that looked like big blocks.

One morning she went into the unemployment office, and the counselor pulled her aside and said he had a new posting for her to see. He had not put the posting in the book yet, because he wanted Mama to have first shot at it. It was a secretarial position for a mid-level manager at Pfizer pharmaceuticals. Mama had fast typing skills and was detail oriented. She applied and was granted an interview. In it she focused on what she could bring to the table and advocated for herself. The interviewer saw potential and took a chance on her. Not only was this job better paying, it had insurance!

On her first day, Mama accidentally hung up on people because she had never used a switchboard. She was terrified she would be told to just go home. But she wasn't, and day by day she grew more comfortable being a secretary. From there she has built a fantastic life for herself. She worked her way up at Pfizer and eventually moved on to other companies. Her last secretarial position was for the CFO of a Fortune 500 home-healthcare company. She is now the Travel and Expense program manager for the same company, owns a beautiful ranch-style home, and drives a Mercedes SUV.

The job at Pfizer changed our life for the better not only financially, but by bringing into our lives the man I call my dad. One of Mama's responsibilities was to plan catering for meetings. She wanted to support local business, so she asked around. Many folks recommended Pete and Tony's Alamo Restaurant, so she hired them for catering. Pete and Tony had opened their restaurant after both working in restaurants for other people. Pete had long since passed, but Tony still owned it, and many of his adult children worked there. Antonio Pablo Moreno and his wife Patricia raised their eight children on two things: the Catholic Church and the Alamo.

Normally James did all the catering, but on the day of the Pfizer job they were double booked. Tony called his oldest son Paul to do the job for him. Paul had struck out on his own, but he knew the job and had a day off, so he grudgingly agreed to help his dad, "one more time." Mama recalls with embarrassment that he showed up too early and she yelled at him, because she wasn't ready to set up the food. But assertive women never deterred him. He kept telling her, "I don't normally work for my father. I bartend at the Olive Garden by the Rangers stadium and am there Saturday nights." They started dating a few weeks later, and he eventually moved in with us. A year later he took me down to the pier at my grandparents' house to ask if it was okay if he proposed to her. I was nine, but he treated me like an adult who had a say in family matters. I asked him if marrying Mama meant I could call him Dad. He said yes.

Dad wanted to marry Mama, but she was still married and we had no clue where Guy was. There were rumors that he might be living in California or Oregon. He had Marine Corps friends in both states. With no actual idea where he was living and working, Mama had to post divorce notices in courthouses in Dallas County before the courts would finally grant her divorce and her case for abandonment. It was either post the notices and wait, or hire a private detective and wait, and the second option was too expensive.

The divorce hearing was finally set, and my parents set out to plan their dream wedding: Valentine's Day at the Fort Worth Botanical Gardens. But when Mama went to court to sign the papers, they stated that she was divorcing Guy Irving Colby IV, instead of Guy Irving Colby V. One extra character, a tiny typo, set their plans back months. They needed a new court date, and Texas law required a month to pass before a recent divorcee could remarry. They were finally married on May 29, 1994. They couldn't get married in the Catholic Church, because Dad had already been married in the Church. So they were married in the First United Methodist Church off Main Street in Grand Prairie. I got to walk Mama down the aisle, and Karen was the flower girl. Mama was twenty-seven when she married Dad, and he was thirty-six, the

same age I was when I began writing this book. The reception was in our backyard, catered by the Alamo, and thirteen months later they gave me a baby sister, Sarah Elizabeth. I wanted a brother and was a bit mad about it. Karen was just mad that Sarah was born on her seventh birthday.

During this time, my mom was moving up the corporate ladder. She now worked for someone with more authority, and her new position had her traveling regularly to New York City to visit Pfizer's corporate headquarters. We begged her each time to take us with her, and each time she said next time. Pfizer eventually closed their Grand Prairie location, so Mama decided to start her own home business to spend more time with Sarah. She worked as an editor out of a converted garage in our back yard that had been our playroom.

Life for our family took a different shape. We had a house with four bedrooms, so no one had to share, and the biggest yard on the block. Life in a two-parent home was much better than life in a single-parent home. Karen and I were in school, and Sarah went to our Aunt Mary's for daycare. With a new family structure came the Moreno family. Most of the eight were married with kids, and there eventually were enough cousins for our own baseball team, plus some. Popo Pat and Popo Tony were devout Catholics, and many Sundays the family took up the last two pews in Mass. After

Mass we would all head to the Popos' house in Arlington for lunch. The cousins would play Mario Bros and Duck Hunt on a small TV in the back bedroom. Or we would hop the fence and go to the school playground that backed up to their yard. But many times I would curl up with a book on the couch and listen to a cousin pluck away at the piano in the front living room. Lunch would be made by Popo Tony, with Dad and other uncles helping. I was much older before I realized that other families don't have the men doing most of the cooking.

My parents were quite involved in our education and made sure we understood its value and importance. They wanted to send me to a private school but had to make do with what they had. The summer after second grade, Mama gave me an algebra workbook meant for eighth graders. She hoped it would keep me busy over the summer, but by the time school started I had taught myself algebra. Mr. Greene, my teacher, didn't believe me and tried to stump me by writing an equation on the board. He was stunned, so he wrote another. I was quite the teacher's pet that year.

My parents quickly tired of me asking loads of questions and, when they no longer were able to give an answer, they gave me a used set of the Encyclopedia Britannica. It frustrated them when I didn't ace a class, because they knew how smart I was. I was years ahead of my peers and by fourth grade was reading at a high school level. I loved getting lost in books, imagining a world where dragons can be slayed.

My mom fought with my teachers when she thought something was unfair. When she found out I was not being allowed to write my report for my pre-AP English class on Tom Landry, she threatened to take it to the school board. I was in sixth grade and the problem, according to my teacher and the principal, was that part of the assignment was to dress up as our hero for open house. They thought having a little girl dress like a man would make people uncomfortable. My teacher kept encouraging me to pick a woman to do a report on. I was hard set on Coach Landry, given that my first choice,

Nolan Ryan, had been given to a classmate. In the end I got to do my report because my mom fought hard enough. She always told me to be a squeaky wheel, make noise, stand up for myself.

They asked that I wear a dress once a year on Easter. I would wear it for Mass but then change into pants as soon as we would get to the Popos' house. They let me wear boy's clothes and cut my hair short. Boy's jeans were better for climbing trees anyway. I played sports, and my childhood friends were mostly boys. My bedroom was decorated with baseball memorabilia, and I spent my weekly allowance on Topps cards, although later it went towards Tiger Beat and Sixteen.

After leaving the Mormon church, I spent the next few years going to church with friends and some family. Mama didn't go to church, and Dad was a Christmas and Easter Catholic. We would join the family for Mass on special occasions like baptisms, first Communions, and holidays, or I would go when I stayed at a cousin's house. In those years my religious education was up to me. I enjoyed going to church with others and learning about different Christian sects. I went to a Lutheran church with one friend, a Baptist church with another, and a Methodist church with yet another. My mother's elderly aunt would take me to her Pentecostal-leaning nondenominational church, and I would jump out of my skin when a member of the congregation erupted into loud tongues and seizing in the aisle. Nanny enrolled us in Vacation Bible School every summer, and we learned all the Bible songs for children.

When Sarah was born, the Popos wanted her baptized immediately, but Mama pushed back. But when Sarah was three the Popos won out and Sarah was baptized. After years of sitting in the back pews and not really paying attention, we were sitting in the front row. Mama had what can only be called a Damascene conversion. She gave me the choice, since I was almost a teenager. I decided to convert to Catholicism and chose the confirmation name Joseph, because Saint Joseph is the patron saint of stepfathers and I wanted to honor Dad.

Mr. Colby never accepted that I left the Mormon Church. Any time we moved, he would call the local Ward to update our address.

As a result, the Ward would send missionaries to our home, which would retraumatize us. This harassment continued even after I left home. The missionaries showed up in Shreveport, hounded me with phone calls in Murfreesboro and Monterey. Each time I would explain to them the mistake.

Sometimes the Ward would understand and stop showing up and calling. But other times they were persistent. I would block the cell phone number, but when a new crop of missionaries arrived, the phone calls would start up again. I had to call the Monterey 1st Ward to threaten a harassment suit to have them remove my name from their roster. Around this time, I had learned that Baren had been arrested for assaulting his daughter and that the family had been gaslighting his young wife, and I decided I was done with the Colby family. I changed my phone number, and I instructed the few Colbys I trusted to never give him my address or new number. The restriction worked until I got married. Mr. Colby managed to find my wedding website and sent us a gift, which I promptly returned.

"I think that is so incredibly sweet to honor Paul like that." Brandy was on speaker, feeding the baby lunch, and I could hear him in the background. I was sitting on the floor with Augie in my lap. He was still so little, and I didn't want him to get any bigger. He still had puppy fur. His full name is Augustus Oliver. Sean picked Augustus from his favorite movie, August Rush, and I picked Oliver from Oliver Twist. We joked that he was named after two orphans.

"My mother was always confused with me. She never knew what to do or to expect."

"Remember when we were on your bachelorette trip in Chicago?"

"Yes! She told the entire group that growing up she thought I was gay!"

"Your mom was really flustered about it, because one of your friends jumped down her throat about it not being a bad thing, being gay."

Mama later clarified with me that she was not worried about me being gay, but about me being gay in the South.

When Sarah was an infant, my dad came to my mom with a wish. He was tired of the restaurant and bar business and wanted to do something new. He wanted to go to college. He had gone in the 1970s but had dropped out, and now he wanted to go back and become a teacher. It was going to be tight, but Mama told him he could. She closed her business and went to work for the Boy Scouts of America in their headquarters and, while I was getting ready for middle school, Dad was enrolling at the University of Texas at Arlington. He was in his late thirties and taking freshman courses with eighteen-year-olds, something I could relate to years later. He worked full time at Landry's Seafood in the West End, in addition to being a full-time dad and a full-time student. He was perpetually exhausted.

We went on family vacations, adopted a dog named Bruiser, and had a glaring of cats. Life was pretty awesome, until Dad decided to adopt us. Guy had resurfaced, and the only way the courts would do it was if he was delinquent on child support for twelve consecutive months. My parents set up child support, knowing Guy would never pay. How the Colbys found out that we were going to be adopted we will never know, but one of them informed Guy. After almost five years of us not knowing whether he was alive, he showed up at the courthouse, eleven and a half months after child support was set up, to sign the wage garnishment papers, and our adoption fell through.

Guy then proceeded to try to be in our lives. He wrote letters begging us not to call our dad Dad. He harassed us with phone calls when he knew my parents were not home. And he frequently threatened Dad that, if anything ever happened to Mama, he would never let Dad have us. My parents worried daily. What if he snatched us again? We walked to school but were forbidden to take shortcuts through the woods. There were to be no chances. The route to school was not an easy one. We had to cross a busy four-lane street. We knew to wait until we got to the top of the hill where, even with the curve in the road, you could see any cars coming. We'd pass the bus barn and turn toward the combined Crockett Elementary and Lee Middle School, separate buildings that shared a cafeteria. We were taught never to get in a car with anyone who offered to give us a ride to school.

Even through all his threats, Guy managed to talk Mama into letting us have dinner with his family. It would be the first time many of them had seen us since we were little, and the Colbys assured us that Baren would not be present. I did not want to go but was reassured we would be safe. Instead, the Colbys made me sit across the table from Baren and listen silently while he bragged about recently having completed his Eagle Scout project. Since Mama was working for the Boy Scouts of America in their corporate office, she made a stink. The Boy Scouts could not have cared less: "Let the boy get his Eagle, since he earned it." You are not supposed to be able to become an Eagle Scout with a criminal record. Today when men brag about obtaining Eagle Scout, it does not impress me. The crowning achievement is forever tarnished. Mama was livid and knew she needed to leave the Boy Scouts and Texas.

As it happened, her old boss Chris Helms was in Memphis with a new Pfizer logistics center, and my Aunt Mary's family had found out that General Motors, where her husband Bill worked, was moving their staff to Memphis and Jackson. Uncle Bill had a choice in his relocation, so Mama told them to pick Memphis and we would move, too. I was one month from finishing eighth grade and did not want to leave. I was excited about going to Grand Prairie High School in the fall and had already picked my classes. I had tried out for the marching band and been accepted. I wanted to play for the Mighty Gophers. My mother had been on their drill team, her brother Sam had been a cheerleader, and her sister Suzie had played clarinet for the marching band. I was eager to continue the tradition. But at fourteen I did not really have a say, and Guy kept writing letters begging me to tell them I wanted to move in with him. Well, that was not going to happen, so I moved to Memphis. Growing up in Dallas taught me how to survive. Coming of age in Memphis taught me how to fight.

CHAPTER 4

I'M OKAY

My parents' decision didn't sit well with me. I was in eighth grade and had a close group of friends. Our school was not small, but the district couldn't pay for multiple honors teachers, so they hired two: one for math and one for everything else. The result was that the seventh- and eighth-grade honors students were with each other most of the day. We became close. I was not used to navigating a schedule or multiple buildings. I was nervous about making friends, apprehensive about shifting schedules, and angry about moving.

I did not know much about Memphis, aside from Elvis and Martin Luther King. A woman in the PTA joked with my mother that we were moving from the city that killed JFK to the city that killed MLK, but I didn't quite understand the reference. It didn't clear up for me upon moving, either. Even after five years in Memphis-area schools, I learned about the connection between the sanitation workers' strike and Dr. King's murder only years later from a podcast.

I was committed to making the move to Memphis as difficult as possible. This required hours of pouting and bargaining. I begged my parents to let me stay with friends so I could finish out the year. The answer was no. I begged them to let me keep my dog, Bruiser. The answer was no. Our house hadn't sold in time, so we were having to move into an apartment where the weight limit on dogs was twenty pounds, and Bruiser was well over that. He was a large mutt I had picked out of a litter when I was seven. I was heartbroken.

On the day of the move I wanted to ride in the moving van with my dad, but it didn't have air conditioning. I didn't want to be anywhere near my mom, since it was her fault we were moving, but I had no choice. I sat in the back seat listening to my Walkman and pouted, wondering anxiously what the coming days would bring. I turned over every scenario, but I knew how they would see me: a nerdy kid with thick glasses and unkempt hair. I worried for the entire eight hours of the drive. When I saw the Mississippi River, I made my mom stop on the Hernando de Soto Bridge for me to throw up. Today the sight of the Memphis bluff and the skyline excites me, but at fourteen it held nothing but fear.

Dad stayed behind to finish his degree. He graduated in 1999, a month after we moved to Memphis. His graduation was our first trip back to Texas. I remember being in the auditorium and swell-

ing with pride. When they called his name, I stood up and shouted, "That's my dad!" and the auditorium erupted in applause. He graduated with a double degree in English and history and had his teaching certificates. Sadly, Tennessee did not recognize a Texas license, so Dad was out of work in Memphis. He went back to waiting tables and taking courses at the University of Memphis to get his Tennessee license.

I had thought a middle school in Texas was a dangerous place, because the school board had chosen to go to school uniforms. Mama was the PTA president, so naturally Dad was also involved. I went to the school board meeting with them to learn about the new uniforms. I heard adults say "increased gang violence" and saw other adults nodding their heads. I assumed they were correct and, in eighth grade, I did lose a schoolmate, A.J. Flores, to gun violence. He had brought his father's gun to a party, the boys were playing with it, and he was shot in the head. His death solidified in my mind that I went to a "bad" school. But then I moved to Kingsbury Middle and High School in Memphis.

It was depressing and scary until I met Brandy, who helped ease the transition. Our teacher sat me at Brandy's table, and by the end of class we had exchanged numbers and she had invited me to stay the night. Her house was across the street from the school, and it became a huge part of my life. If I was in trouble at home, I always had a spot on the Brantleys' couch.

I learned fast what it meant to be perceived as a privileged white kid in an urban school. My first lesson was in the first hour of my first class, when I walked into Pre-AP history and thought I had read the schedule wrong. I am ashamed to admit that I went back to the school counselor to confirm my schedule. I went back to class and apologized for being lost. I had thought I was in the wrong class because I was the only white kid there. The next month was a series of lessons, and I failed each one. I was miserable and missed my friends in Texas but looked forward to summer break. Dad was taking us on a huge road trip to visit family.

Mama was staying behind, because she needed to get our new townhouse in order and was starting her new job. It was the coolest and most memorable trip, because I got to sit in the front seat and navigate. MapQuest was a new thing, but Dad wanted to teach me how to read a paper map. We were visiting family and friends in Wisconsin, Michigan, and Missouri. I got to decide the routes we took, which is how we ended up driving through cornfields in Iowa. My instructions were to find an interesting route or one we hadn't driven before. I remember unfolding the map on Uncle Mark's table in St. Joseph, Michigan, poring over the tiny writing to glean the perfect route to Jamestown, Missouri. As it happens, Iowa is relatively boring when you're fourteen. But I remember how great it felt that Dad thought of me as an adult capable of making informed decisions.

Returning to Memphis and starting high school was hell. Brandy knew what it was like. Her father was a Navy Seabee with orders to the local base in Millington, north of Memphis, and she had been to more schools than I had. Both of us are glad that our high school years kept us in the same city, and we quickly became best friends. I often wonder if the only reason Brandy and I clung together in that hellscape was that we were among the few white kids in the school. Whatever the reason, she was a huge part of my teenage years and has remained my best friend ever since.

Most nerdy, artistic people consider high school hell, but what I went through at Kingsbury rivaled my later experiences in the military. In 1999, Brandy and I were both smart-mouthed girls who knew we were meant for bigger things. We stuck together through the bullying, hormones, and terrible boyfriends. Many times, when the bullying got too bad or I was just trying to find someplace safe to hide until the bus came, I would skip class and watch TV at Brandy's house. She wasn't as brave as I was about skipping class, but she always gave me a key. Her parents both worked, so there was little chance of getting caught. My bus driver once saw me darting back across the street and joked with me when I jumped on his bus. When the bullying on the bus got so bad that I was assaulted, my parents worked out an arrangement with the Brantleys to let me hang out until they could pick me up. It was out of the way, but they had already planned on moving me to a new school.

In my first month I realized that my English teacher didn't know my name, and I wasn't the kind of kid who sat quietly in the back. I was the brainy, know-it-all white kid who raised her hand and answered every question. And the teacher still didn't know my name. So I stopped going except when there was a test. My morning bus was always late and sometimes didn't show up, which meant I was almost always late to homeroom. If you were late to homeroom you were counted absent, even if you showed up to the rest of your classes. I figured since I was already marked as absent, I would just pick and choose which classes I went to.

If I did happen to make it to homeroom, I had a plan B to get out of my classes. I had made copies of a blank excuse slip signed by my band teacher. All the band kids did this, and Mr. Kennedy was too stoned to care. Band at Kingsbury was more a group of bullied kids than a group of musicians. Only fifteen of us actually knew how to play instruments. I had learned to play the alto sax the summer before. I had always thought the saxophone was cooler than the clarinet and was overjoyed when my parents let me switch. Like the innocent kid I was, I used my free time from skipping class to hide out practicing in the band hall's practice rooms. That is, until one of the seniors I shared a duet with asked if I wanted to practice, then turned off the lights and groped me. I escaped, and I did not allow myself to be alone around him again. But that disrupted the safety of the practice rooms, and I had to find other places to hide. Trial and error led me to the technology classrooms, and I had fun playing around with the CAD programs. The irony was that I was skipping class to go to a different class. But none of the adults seemed to notice an extra kid in their classroom. Either that, or they let me stay because I didn't cause trouble.

I didn't skip all my classes. I attended the ones I found interesting, or in which the teacher found interest in us. Or I attended out of spite. My geometry teacher told me, on the first day, to "sit in the back of the class" because she "didn't have time to explain anything to me twice." I was the youngest in the class, a freshman, and there were seniors taking it for the third time. I was angry at this woman for automatically assuming I was worthless, so I aced every test but sat in the back and refused to speak, even when called upon. My favorite class was business strategies, taught by my favorite teacher, Coach Brown. When I needed to find after-school activities to avoid having to ride the bus, Coach suggested I be the team statistician for girls' basketball, which he coached. I didn't know a thing about basketball but gladly learned if it meant I wouldn't have to ride the bus.

My first test was the all-city tournament at the Pyramid, which was still a basketball arena. I was going to get to spend an entire day there. But as we got on the bus my period started, and I was too embarrassed to ask the other girls for a tampon. I kept making excuses to get up and stuff more toilet paper in my underwear and pray. My only saving grace was that the school color was maroon, and I was wearing the team jump suit. When we got back to school late that night I quietly changed, stuffed my soiled pants as far down into the hamper as possible, and hoped no one would notice.

As luck would have it, the player whose turn it was to do the washing was the biggest and meanest senior on the team. She quickly figured out it was me, and I became her favorite target. For weeks she followed me around school, throwing tampons at my head, calling me a "nasty girl" and "white trash." She got other kids to join in, and I spent many of those days crying in the bathroom. I begged my parents to let me quit being the team statistician, and they refused. I knew that if I told them my reasons, they would have raised hell. But I also knew that to survive I would have to fight my own battles. A few weeks later, things came to a head. We had lost miserably again, and my tormentor was worse when she was in a particularly foul mood. She began throwing basketballs at my head and taunting me with her usual insults. I was gathering my things in the stands, a few rows up from the court, and I snapped. I leapt over the rows of bleachers onto her back and punched her in the head, as she screamed for someone to get me off her.

This was not "kids being kids." This was an adult senior with gang connections terrorizing and verbally assaulting a child a hundred pounds lighter and two feet shorter, and I had reached my breaking point. Coach Brown pulled me off her, and the other girls stood around in disbelief. Coach Brown calmed me down, then told me that he was supposed to report me for fighting, but that if he did, I would be expelled, and he didn't think that would be fair. For weeks he had been trying to get her to stop, but nothing had worked. His hands were tied, since I had not reported the bullying. He asked now if I wanted to report her, and I told him no. Coach Brown also saved me by not telling my parents. They had raised me to believe that fighting is never the right option, but they had never been teenagers in an inner-city high school.

Not only did the senior stop bullying me, but she spread the word to not mess with the "fucking psycho" little white girl. The rest of my year at Kingsbury was uneventful, and for my sophomore year my parents moved me to the suburbs.

CHAPTER 5

Half of My Hometown

Every public high school in Memphis had a magnet school attached. Kingsbury was the technology school. White Station, where my cousins went, was the honors school. Overton, where I wanted to go, was the arts school. My band director had arranged for me to have an interview with their band director, and I was excited. There was just one flaw in the Memphis City School Plan: no busing system. Like so many programs, it was a great idea on paper but failed miserably in its implementation. There was no way for a kid like me, who had two working parents, to go to Overton without taking the awful city buses. The flaw affected not just me but kids like Brandy, who should have been at White Station. It ended up being worse than the private schools about taking talent out of a neighborhood. It upheld the children of the Memphis elite and left the rest of us behind. Moving to a Shelby County school system was better for me, but I felt awful for the few friends I left behind.

The rest of high school was relatively uneventful. I was still the nerdy band girl but, from being a target, I became mostly invisible. I liked being invisible. I never tried out for solos, barely memorized my music, didn't exert myself in any classes. I made decent grades but didn't try. Kingsbury had taught me that to survive you have to be unremarkable. I did, however, manage to get suspended for fighting in the second week of band camp. My parents were furious because I was going to miss the first few days of my sophomore year, but I was pleased with myself.

Alexis was a sophomore but the size of a senior and mean to the bone. I was attempting to memorize my steps so Mr. Cooke would stop screaming at me through the loudspeaker. I had stayed behind with another sax player to try to do them correctly, and by the time we made it back to the band hall, most students were gone. Alexis had a freshman flute player cornered by the back door and was berating him with horrible slurs because she thought he was gay for playing the flute, and he was crying. I demanded that she leave him alone. Her response was to try to hit my face, so I raised my hands in protection. That was the moment Mr. Cooke walked out of the band hall and, because I had protected myself, I was also suspended. My parents raised me to always defend the defenseless, so I was confused that they were upset with me. But I was glad about the choice I had made.

I had music to look forward to, but marching band was incredibly stressful. The joy I found in playing an instrument was zapped out of me by an adult who held on to antiquated teaching methods. Mr. Cooke was one of those music teachers that led with fear, and he thought that made him a good teacher. Maybe some people respond to fear, but it gave me stage fright. I hated negative attention, and I was constantly messing up, which caused more negative attention.

Sophomore year was my first year in marching band, since that

first year at Kingsbury didn't count, and I always felt a year behind in learning how to march. The piece we were playing had the saxophone section in the very front, on the fifty-yard line, in full view of the judges. Every mistake would be visible, so it had to be perfect. For this part, the whole band stopped for a short period to play and then would step off. Show band is all about the wow factor, so to make it even more difficult we were stepping off on an offbeat, but to make it work it had to be in unison. It was an impressive set, and it did win us awards at competition. But that fall I just wasn't getting it.

My nerves were shot, and I was trying as hard as I could but getting it wrong every time. I would step off a beat too soon or too late. The more I thought about it, the worse it got. Even now I can see the loop the saxes made toward the front, and feel the knot in my stomach. We paused in the front, and I wouldn't even play. I would move my fingers and count in my head and pray I got it right, which I wouldn't. Practice would stop, and Mr. Cooke would scream at me through his megaphone. As if that were not embarrassing enough, many times the band would be practicing at the same time as the football team, and they would hear the yelling. He would use my full name, Stesha Anne, which made the football players roar with laughter. The band would groan, and we would start over. For weeks I couldn't get anything right. My section leaders, two seniors, would shake their heads, and two of the freshmen would tell me that they got it correct so I should, too. I felt alone in my own section and told my friend Mike that I wanted to drop band. Mike was a senior and a section leader for the French horns. He asked me to stay to the end of the week, and I agreed. But I walked home from practice that day mentally figuring out how to tell my parents I wanted to quit, after all the years of music lessons.

At the next practice something happened to change my mind: Mr. Cooke apologized, on the loudspeaker, in front of everyone. I was shocked but still anxious. I missed the step, again, and for a split second I braced myself for the screaming, but it never came, and I realized the band was still marching. I regained my steps and kept going. On the next move through I finally got it right, and it felt incredible. Not being the main focus gave me the chance to get it right. Later I found out that Mike and several other section leaders had told Mr. Cooke that if I dropped out of band, they would too. They asked him to back off and give me a chance. He must have known they were serious, and I thank them for it. I never did learn how to play while marching; it was too much pressure to do two things at once. But that also meant that I never went for the solos. I did everything I could to avoid becoming a target.

The environment at Bartlett allowed me to let my guard down. The kids were not as bad, for the most part, and the teachers knew my name. Our band won awards, and I was proud to be part of something bigger than myself. I was involved in church youth group, played summer softball, had an after-school job, and dated a few guys. But I never dealt with my underlying trauma, and that made me anxious, awkward, and ill-tempered. Sometimes I wonder what my teenage years would have been like if I had been given the tools to address my mental health properly.

One day Mama was volunteering at Youth Villages, painting classroom walls, when she overheard the principal mention that they were hiring teachers. She asked about licensing and learned that only a bachelor's degree was required. Dad interviewed and was hired on.

Youth Villages was a different sort of school. It was a residential treatment facility, and all the students were court ordered to attend. They were separated into cottages, based on the reasons they were there. The lower part of the cottage was a classroom, and the upper half was the living quarters. My dad's first teaching assignment was in special education. The boys in his classroom had all committed sex crimes, but they were also so mentally handicapped that the court felt they didn't understand the nature of their crime. It was no surprise to my dad that the boys had all been victims as well. Part of their education was counseling, so they would not repeat their crimes when they rejoined society.

Dad stayed in that classroom for seven years. He also continued with his courses at the University of Memphis, because he did want to have his license. He had wanted to be a history teacher and work in the public school system. He was enrolled in the master's program and changed his major to special education. When he received his master's, in December 2006, I was a week from graduating from Marine boot camp. The day of his graduation party fell on Senior Sunday, when recruits are allowed a few hours of freedom. After hitting the PX for junk food, I sat on the concrete floor of a room lined with pay phones and waited to call home to congratulate him.

The tragedy of September 11, 2001 took place early in our junior year. I remember watching the attack on the TV in my German classroom. One of the other students was flipping through the channels and many of the boys were sitting in the back, playing Magic the Gathering. I caught a glimpse of a building on fire and yelled for the guy to go back. The twenty of us sat in silence. Herr Beger was my favorite teacher. He had been an Army linguist during the Cold War, and he regaled us with stories of being stationed in Germany. I remember more about those stories than I do actual German. Visiting recently on a trip through Memphis, his wife Jane told me that I was not his only former student to have ended up at the Defense Language Institute, as he had. It was fitting that I was in his classroom that day. Not quite five years later, I raised my hand to join the Marines. Herr Beger knew what those planes meant, and he cried. Brandy and I both feared what that meant for her father, who was a reservist. His unit was never called up, but he volunteered to go to active duty. He went to Afghanistan and Iraq and came home a different man.

After that day, high school took on a different feeling. We were old enough to enlist but too young to grasp the gravity of war. We all wanted to get payback and go blow shit up and hunt down terrorists. Seeing the recruiters on campus took on a new meaning. Older friends were enlisting and leaving home, but we were still children and had a few more years of school. Brandy and I continued our shenanigans, learned to drive, had crushes on boys whose names are now lost to time. I was one of the few who had my own car. My mother had gotten a new van and handed down her green Ford Escort hatchback. In the summers several friends would hide under the retractable vinyl cover to sneak into the drive-in on Summer Avenue. It was a double feature and you paid per car.

Senior year approached and we all started making plans. Brandy set her sights on the University of Tennessee, the flagship campus in Knoxville. For as long as I could remember, I had wanted to go to Texas A&M. I just knew I would be accepted and had a wardrobe of nothing but Aggie gear. I was going to join the Corps of Cadets and play for the Aggieland Band. In October my parents took me to College Station to participate in Stay the Night with the Corps. Prospective students shadowed sophomores to class, ate with them and, in my case, attended band practice.

I learned the traditions, sang the songs, and was convinced I belonged there. I asked questions of the other Marine ROTC students and got to witness the freshmen, or Fish, get quarter decked. Every Monday the Fish would line the dorm halls and get a taste of boot camp, with the sophomores playing the role of drill instructor. There was yelling, push-ups, uniform inspections, and more push-ups. Then it was over, and everyone went on their way to their next place of duty. Out-of-state tuition cost more than my father's annual salary, but my parents were committed to sending me whatever the cost.

I submitted my application as early as I could and awaited my acceptance letter. Fall turned to winter and my other friends got their early acceptance letters from the University of Memphis, Christian Brothers University, the University of Tennessee, and Ole Miss. One was accepted at Notre Dame, another at Harvard. Some had letters from senators and were headed to the military academies. And still I waited for my letter. We would check online and see the school was still waiting on my transcripts. I would ask my guidance counselor to send my transcripts again, and yet when I went online it was still waiting on my transcripts.

My parents didn't want to step in, because they wanted me to learn independence. I was going to be in Texas and hours away from everyone I knew, and I needed to be able to take care of myself. But by spring, Mama was frustrated and called the admissions office. They had been getting my transcripts, but they were not official. They needed the seal. I went back to the counselor and asked why the transcripts were not official. The answer was that they sent the seal only to the military academies, unless a student requested it and paid five dollars.

The official transcripts arrived days after the application window closed. My parents and I wrote a letter. My vice-principal and the counselor wrote letters explaining the mistake and imploring A&M to give me an exemption. The university responded by stating that over 40,000 students had been able to submit their full applications on time, and they were not going to make an exception. I was devastated. I had put all my eggs in one basket and was at a loss. I had no safety schools. I quickly scrambled and applied to other schools whose application windows had not yet closed, and was accepted to Middle Tennessee State University.

Shortly before my sixteenth birthday Guy tried to reconnect, saying he was getting remarried and wanted me and Karen in the wedding. Mama reluctantly agreed, and we went back to Texas for an awkward meeting with our new step siblings, Casey and Jennifer. Guy's new wife, Michelle, insisted we call her Mom, and Guy was upset when we declined. Mama and Dad made him promise not to drink while we were there, a promise he promptly broke. In fact, the night before his wedding he got plastered and ran out of beer. He forced me to drive him to the store to get more beer and to drive back. I reminded him that I was not yet sixteen and did not have a license. He waved this off and forced me to drive anyway. I was terrified. I did not tell my parents about his drinking, because I knew they would have came to get us and it would have caused a scene.

He came to my graduation and I was incredibly nervous, walking on eggshells. At my party he was rude to my mother's friends and tried to make it all about him. He loudly announced that he didn't want to watch the slideshow Mama had made because he "doubted he would be in it." As it was, there were more pictures of him and me than of my dad and me. When I called my dad Dad, Guy exclaimed that Paul was not my real father and I should call him Dad. My Aunt Mary laid into him, yelling that real fathers stick around to raise their kids, and Guy angrily stormed out.

"Man, I remember that. I felt so bad for you. Dad wanted to slug him for behaving so badly."

"I was mortified. I hated that he spoiled a day that was about me by making it about him."

I was walking back and forth in the yard, letting the boys out again. The day was warmer than usual, and I had traded my hoodie for a t-shirt. I don't think this one was clean, but at least it didn't smell too bad. This time I didn't put my shoes on, and the stones in the walkway were warm on my bare feet.

"I should have realized it was an omen. That whole summer was nuts."

My boyfriend had cheated on me with his debate partner, and I was having difficulty remaking myself after the year he had spent tearing me down. He would tell me I was stupid, and I believed him because he was the one in a private school and his parents were college educated. He was the one who was in Model UN and had college scholarships and his whole life ahead of him. I was, as he put it, destined always to be the daughter of a secretary. He dumped me right before prom and graduation. One of my friends offered to set me up with his best friend. I had known Bobby for years, and had no reason not to trust him when he told me Adam was interested in me. Bobby told me Adam was shy, so I needed to pursue him. He said Adam didn't have caller ID, so I always needed to leave a message. He told me he liked it when women took the initiative.

Turns out it was all a joke that neither Adam nor I was in on. Adam's mother told Bobby's mother I was stalking Adam and making him uncomfortable. My mother was mortified when Bobby's mother cornered her at a church function, saying I had to leave Adam alone. I was mortified because all these adults I had babysat for for years were quick to believe I was a stalker. I was devastated that my mother believed their side, refused to listen to what I had to say, and took my cellphone away. I shut down and never said another word to those church ladies. I spent the next month working every shift I could, and in August I was more than happy when I got in my car and drove four hours to Murfreesboro.

CHAPTER 6

GIRL GOIN' NOWHERE

I had wanted to go into the Marines right away, but my parents persuaded me to go to college first. I had wanted to go to A&M and had set my sights on being an officer, and I had no real desire to go elsewhere. I tried to convince them I could use the GI Bill, and they thought it was a hoax to get me to enlist. I went grudgingly to Middle Tennessee State. I wanted to be an architect but failed Calculus 3. By May I had changed my degree plan four times. I was lost. I majored in partying. I found that I loved beer and dating. I wasn't sleeping with any of them, because I was terrified of getting knocked up. Even though I wasn't having sex, one boy had convinced himself that I was pregnant with his child and told everyone at the Catholic Student Center that I had gone home during spring break to have an abortion. Worse was that they believed him and told me to stop coming to the center. Yet again I felt lost and friendless.

By May 2004 the college formally gave me the boot. I didn't want to tell my parents, so instead I made the mature choice to move to Shreveport, Louisiana with a boy I barely knew who was in the Air Force. We got an apartment close to base. It wasn't the best neighborhood, and rent was only $400 a month. I had a part-time job as a substitute teacher at St. Joseph Catholic School and also worked in the aftercare program for three- to five-year-olds. When school let out for the summer I worked as a nanny, and two months of that swore me off kids for a decade.

Daniel was from Nassau County on Long Island, and we visited his family twice. On the first visit his little Italian grandmother insulted my cooking because Daniel was so thin. "Whose fault is that?" I retorted. "You and his mother never let him in the kitchen and told him cooking is a woman's job." Once I was visiting my parents while Daniel had stayed in Shreveport, and while Mama and I were sitting at the table, Daniel called to ask for my help. She could only hear my side of the conversation: "Okay, you open the packages and put them in the jug. No, it's on the shelf by the fridge. Okay, next add two cups of sugar. It's in the pantry. Now add water. It needs to be warm to melt the sugar. No, you don't need to boil it. Yes, from the tap is fine. Now you stir it."

I got off the phone and Mama stared at me. "Did you just have to walk him through making Kool-Aid?" I sighed. "He says the directions were too small."

On our first visit to his family, we went into the city and his grandmother got us lost. She was reading the subway map incorrectly, and we got on the wrong train. I had been looking at the map and pointed out that we were going the wrong way. She whipped around and exclaimed that she had grown up in Queens and could read the subway map better than a "little Southern girl." While she was arguing with me and trying to figure out how to get to where we needed to go, a local with a thick New York accent said, "Listen to the kid! She's telling you the right way to go." I got the impression she didn't like me very much.

On our second trip I wanted to go into the city, but Daniel's family didn't want to take me. Daniel hated the city and told me he had already taken me and didn't want to do it again. We were only there for four days, and he wanted to spent time with his old friends. I persuaded his mom to drop me off at the Hempstead station and took the Long Island Rail Road to Penn Station. I told her when I would be taking the train back, and she agreed to pick me up. I was so excited to be able to explore exactly as I wanted to. After buying the tickets I had only fifteen dollars left, so I knew I needed to walk everywhere. I didn't need any souvenirs and had my point-and-click camera.

My mother happened to call while I was on the train, and I told her I would likely lose signal soon. She told me to tell Daniel she said hi, and I informed her that I was by myself. She freaked out that her twenty-year-old baby was going to be by herself in the big city. I laughed and reminded her that she often came to New York alone. I also reminded her that teenagers ride the trains every day with little trouble. I told her I had grown up watching NYPD Blue and knew better than to go down strange alleys. Still, she called me every hour to make sure I hadn't been mugged.

I was very obviously a tourist, staring at the big buildings and taking pictures of everything. I couldn't afford to go up the Empire State Building and was happy to see it from the outside. I walked around and visited all the spots I had seen in movies. I fell in love with Manhattan, dreamed of one day living there, vowed to persuade Daniel to move there after the Air Force. I was naïve enough to think I could persuade him to do anything.

Daniel was nice but not for me in the long run. After a year I saw that and decided to return to MTSU. I left Daniel and our dog Hershey behind and never turned around. Sadly, I missed the dog more than the man.

"I honestly did not remember you living in Louisiana. Where on earth was I?"

"It's all good. You were in Knoxville and had your hands full with that douchebag you started dating senior year."

"Oh yeah. I've blocked that whole time out of my memory. We don't speak his name."

I laughed with her. "Hey, I have those boys I wish I had never dated. I can just be thankful they never knocked me up."

"Agreed! I'm glad Douchebag and I never became parents together."

We laughed and talked for a minute about the boys whose names we can almost remember and how we always thought we were in love. Greyson pawed at my leg, and I realized his water bowl was empty. I filled it and he drank it fast. I felt guilty and wondered when I had last given them water.

That year in Shreveport hadn't done much to mature me, though. If given the option, I still chose partying and skipping class. I was slightly older, so I hung out with older students, including an Army veteran who looked exactly like Matthew McConaughey, drawl and all. Sadly, a few parties into the semester I attracted the attention of another former soldier. Mark escorted me back to my dorm room and locked the door, and I promptly passed out on my bed. If my roommate hadn't seen him leave the party with me, it might have been worse. She and a few friends were on our heels and banged on the door hard enough to wake me up. I saw him naked and on top of me and screamed. A suitemate came bursting in from our shared bathroom, and we girls spent the night huddled together, talking and crying. I was disgusted with myself and wondered why he would have chosen me to latch on to. I blamed myself and decided not to report it; I had seen what happened when friends had reported their campus assaults.

One of those was my roommate. A guy we partied with had locked her in his car, and she didn't escape until after it was over. She and I called the campus police. They told her that since she had gotten into the car with him, they could do nothing. I was already on my way to another academic suspension and didn't care what happened to me, so I took my baseball bat to his new BMW and waited for the retaliation. It never came. When he called his father to tell him about the car, his father chose to pull him out of school. MTSU was his third college. I thanked my lucky stars.

By the end of Thanksgiving break, I realized I needed an actionable plan. I didn't want to admit to my parents that I had failed, and I had no guy to fall back on. So I decided that my best option was the military. I knew I wanted to be a linguist. I was smart enough, and if it was a military school, I would not be able to skip class. I spoke to the Air Force first and was honest about my partying and drug use. They asked me to leave. It wasn't like I was stupid enough to continue using drugs. I just gave them an honest answer, because lying is worse.

The Navy told me women don't serve on ships, and that I would be on land the entire time. I called them on their lie and left of my own accord. The Army told me they didn't have any linguists, and that I needed to sign an open contract. I laughed in their face and walked out. The Marines in that office in Murfreesboro wouldn't give me the time of day, because I was sixty pounds overweight. The staff sergeant told me he didn't have the time to babysit me, only for me to fail. It was his dismissal that made me determined to be a Marine. I figured I would just go to another office when I got to Memphis and keep knocking on doors until someone said yes.

Now it was time to face my parents. I went home for Christmas break, started talking to a recruiter, and worked on a plan to drop sixty pounds. I met several times with the recruiter and was adamant that I would join only if he got me a spot at the Defense Language Institute in Monterey, California. The night before I was due to return to MTSU was when I chose to tell my parents that instead I was going into the Marines. As expected, there was shouting. My shocked mother blurted out: "You can't join the Marines. You're fat!"

Even though I didn't leave for Parris Island until the end of September, I actually enlisted in April 2006, five months earlier. I was at MEPS (Military Entrance Processing Station) doing the physical and the duck walk and all the other embarrassing exercises they make you do in your underwear, and I felt out of place. I was good at hiding my fat rolls, but when you're standing in your bra and panties in a room with thirty other women, it's impossible. I was 145 pounds, five over the limit for my height, but the staff sergeant in my recruiting office was dating the intake sergeant, and she had agreed to fudge my official weight. Their justification for the ruse was that I still had months until boot camp and had time to lose the last five pounds.

Most people, when they enlist, go to boot camp right away. They walk in the office, tell the recruiter they want to enlist, take the ASVAB (Armed Services Vocational Aptitude Battery), then off they go. But since I was adamant that I would not accept any contract unless I had a spot at DLI, I had time. Those spots are rare and hard to come by. There are extra tests and conversations. They tried to talk me out of it by telling me how hard the schoolhouse is and how hard it is to get promoted in the field. But I knew what I wanted and, since I had the highest score in Tennessee that year on the DLAB (Defense Language Aptitude Battery), I got what I wanted. In the end my recruiter traded a language school spot for twenty infantry spots with a recruiter in rural Arkansas. I had my spot and my ship date and an entire summer to prepare.

I was twenty-one, living back at home in Memphis, and working at a city baseball program for the parks and recreation department. It was a few miles from my parents' house, and I could rollerblade or bike to work. Once a week I went to the recruiting station with the rest of the poolies who had already committed to joining the Corps but had to wait for boot camp. Some had to lose weight. Some had

to train harder to pass the initial physical fitness test. Some had to study to pass the ASVAB. What I lacked in speed on my three-mile, I made up for in tutoring the poolies. The minimum score on the ASVAB to join the Marines is 32. My score was 98. Some of the poolies could barely make an 18, and that was with a high school diploma. Rather an indictment of the education system in Memphis, if you ask me.

I had my summer planned out and looked forward to the end of September. Then the other shoe dropped. One Sunday evening in

July I had come back home, tired from the baseball field, and Dad and I got into a fight. He felt I was not pulling my weight around the house, and I felt he was asking too much of me, given that I was working back-to-back shifts and paying rent. I had missed Mass that morning and left the house shortly before breakfast. There was a tournament, and I was opening the concession stands. My youngest sister Sarah had decided to make everyone French toast before Mass, and that evening the dishes were still in the sink. When I got home, instead of immediately doing the dishes from a meal I hadn't eaten, I went up to my room to relax. My dad felt this was the last straw, and the yelling started. I yelled back, and soon fists were being thrown. I called a friend to get me and walked out, resolved not to return.

My friend drove me to the Brantleys', and they took me in. Brandy's family had always felt like a second home, and now I was crashing on their couch. The downside was that it was ten miles from work and I didn't have a car. Brandy and I worked together, so we could sometimes ride together, but when I worked a different shift, I rode my bike. I would leave early and come home late. I was exhausted, but it helped me lose weight. You can forget that Memphis has hills until you're on a bike. Memphis, in 2005, was not bike friendly and I had to navigate busy streets. The busiest was Covington Pike. It's amazing I didn't get hit by a car.

During those few months, I didn't speak to my parents. I was waiting on an apology from my dad for raising his hand and from my mom for taking his side. One of those mornings, as I was riding to work, my mom passed me on my bike. I didn't know she was there. She cried the rest of the way to work. By the end of the summer, I did move back in with my parents, and I'm forever grateful for the time I had with the Brantleys.

The summer went by fast and, before I knew it, it was time to go to Parris Island.

PART TWO

ONE LESS DAY

CHAPTER 7

BUILD A BITCH

On September 24, 2006, a little over five years after that day in German Club, I raised my hand to be sworn into the Marines. I kissed my parents goodbye and said I would see them in three months. I was put on a plane headed directly for South Carolina. From the airport we got onto a bus with several drill instructors and were told to put our heads down. Some slept, but I was too excited and nervous. Eventually the bus pulled up in front of a building and the doors opened. That's when the screaming started.

We all clumsily got off the bus, disoriented. Which way is north? Why am I being screamed at? Why is my face wet? Is it raining or is that spit? Through the screams, shouts, and cries we each found our spot on the yellow footprints in front of the intake building. Seventeen years later, I could still point out mine. Then we were shuffled into the building to drop off our civilian clothes and pick up our uniforms. They had no name tapes yet; those would come after graduating. Why waste good embroidery on someone who might wash out?

We got our hygiene kits and manuals and underwear. It was a shuffle around open bins; we took one of each. If you skipped one or grabbed two, you were screamed at. We picked up a stenciling kit and were told to use it to label all our clothes and the small, camouflaged bag with our last name. For two days we were in the intake building, and the drill instructors alternated between screaming at us and leaving us alone in a classroom for hours. We spent those days using our ink kits and stenciling our names on our gear. All the gear was identical and smelled of starch and new plastic. When we finally got to a rack we were sleep-deprived, exhausted, and sore. The multiple rounds of shots left our arms black and blue.

I am not a huge fan of needles and have to look the other way when I have my blood drawn. We stood in a straight line and had corpsmen on either side giving us cocktails of vaccines and, in that moment, I was more terrified of the onlooking drill instructors than I was of the needles. I steeled myself to not flinch and shuffled away when the deed was done. We had recruits coming from all over the world, and most of us got sick in the first week. Two women never got better and were sent home before boot camp even started. At the end of the week, we met our real drill instructors.

We had four. One kill hat, one drill hat, one senior, one extra. The extra one was training and shadowing the drill hat. When our first drill hat left, we were sad. We all wished the kill hat would leave. Sergeant Martinez was a little asshole with a Napoleon complex. We all hated her. But when my parents came for graduation and Mama joked about shitting in her pillowcase, I jumped to her defense. I would love to have a beer with her today, though I would probably still be scared shitless if she started yelling. Those four women taught us everything we needed to learn as potential Marines.

Not everyone made it. Many washed out, including the one from Murfreesboro. Her recruiter had been the one who dismissed me, and I found it poetic justice that his choice couldn't pass the rifle range.

She was cycled down to another company. If you can't pass something you're given two more chances, but you have to go to another platoon.

We also got some recycles. One of these was PFC Shepherd. She had been in three other platoons. She knew her stuff and could shoot well. Her bad luck was her health. By the time she came to us, she didn't care and did the bare minimum. She had been on the island for a year and a half and just wanted to see her parents, who had been kept away even when she had surgery on her leg. No one can blame her but, in the moment, we viewed her as "less than" and a "shit bag" for not trying harder.

She did graduate and went on with us to MCT (Marine Combat Training). She continued to do the bare minimum, and the group was punished. I remember her getting chewed out over and over, and I was just happy the pressure was off me for a change. We humped for miles and would march in two lines, one on each side of the trail. Shepherd and I were in first platoon, so we were at the front of the company. If you had to fall out, you would move to the middle of the trail. Inevitably Shepherd fell out, and after the first time our instructor was fed up. The sergeant would march behind her, yelling and calling her all sorts of ugly names. The company would march past and, when Shepherd got to the end of fourth platoon, the company would stop, and the sergeant would march Shepherd back to the front of first platoon and the hump would continue. This lasted for miles.

My memories of boot camp are disjointed. To this day I can't tell you in what order we did things, or even the names of the other women. I can still tell you who the Grand Ole Man was: Archibald Henderson. Or who the First Woman Marine was: Opha May Johnson. I know the names of the only two Marines to have received two Medals of Honor: Smedley Butler and Dan Daly. And I can name the location where the Marine Corps was founded: Tun Tavern, Philadelphia, November 10, 1775. I knew all the calls and answers to every bit of Marine Corps lore.

I also remember when our company commander sat us down and told us this was going to be the very last time we would be surrounded by so many women. She told us about her time in Iraq, commanding a unit of men and having a tent all to herself. Many of us were going to be the only female in our shops. She told us that, because the Corps was so small, our mistakes and accomplishments would follow us for our whole career. Everyone was connected to everyone else, and being transferred to a new unit was a game of Six Degrees of Kevin Bacon. She warned us to not be "barracks whores," and that our male counterparts were not likely to accept us. In their eyes you were either a bitch or a whore. There were going to be whispers of having daddy issues or being a lesbian. She assured us there is no changing their perception of you, and admonished us to be the best in every shop. We did not have the luxury of being second best.

I remember a few people, like my bunkmate, Dale Cooey. At MEPS she had been given orders to San Diego, and she kept arguing with them about what her orders should be. When she finally screamed "I have a fucking vagina!" the clerk realized their error. In 2006, women went only to Parris Island; today the Marines have had a few female platoons graduate from San Diego. Sadly, Dale broke her leg on the Crucible, a three-day field exercise at the tail end of boot camp. If you passed the Crucible, you could earn the title "Marine." Dale's leg never healed properly, and a year later she was medically discharged. She never left Parris Island and never saw the fleet.

One woman, barely eighteen, had run away from an abusive father to join the Marines. Her family had no idea she was in South Carolina. Another was from Rio de Janeiro and couldn't go home between boot camp and combat training because the mass protesting there of civil rights issues and police brutality had turned to riots. She had to scramble to find somewhere to go, and I think she went home with one of the other ladies. Another woman was prior enlisted Army and had made the rank of sergeant and even been deployed. The Marines make prior service folks go through boot camp again. It was no surprise that she became our guide.

One Marine was transferred to our platoon because there were rumors in her other platoon that she was a lesbian. No one wanted to befriend her, and the homophobia spread. Many women left behind children and cried at night, missing their babies. One woman was from Papua New Guinea and had the most interesting accent. During hand-to-hand combat, she came running at her opponent emitting a hair-raising scream. When our drill instructor asked what she was doing, she responded, "It is my war cry, ma'am." We all stifled laughter.

Every day was roughly the same thing: classes and training all day, and at night a quick shower. After our showers was mail call, and after that we had an hour of free time, called Senior Drill Instructor Square Away Time. During mail call we would anxiously wait for our name to be called, hoping for something from the outside world. Most of the time it was letters, but sometimes one of us would get a care package. They would have to stand in a line in the front of the squad bay to have it inspected. Some items were contraband and thrown out. For each piece of contraband, you owed the drill instructor ten push-ups. I was approved to have my parents send me potassium pills, as the constant physical activity and limited nutrition gave me terrible charlie horses.

My mother had gotten all her friends to send me post cards from all over the U.S., and it seemed as if I was getting something nightly. I still have those post cards, and every few years I pull them out of their storage box. Some women received nothing, so Mama would send them post cards too.

On one of these mail calls, I received a nice long letter from Brandy. She wrote about how life was going and how her father's SeaBee unit was rumored to be activating for Iraq and he was itching to go. He told the family that if he didn't get called up, he would volunteer. She ended the letter by reminding me of a failed date, junior year, with a boy from Kingsbury. Paul was a year ahead of us, and I knew him through a drummer in our band. Everyone knew Paul had a crush on Brandy, so we persuaded her to go on a date with him. Their date fizzled, and she always said afterward that he wasn't for her. Well, Brandy now mentioned, she had decided to give him another chance, and they had been dating for a month. I responded, wishing her well.

Another letter came from Karen, saying she had decided to take a job in Florida, working for Disney World. It was a six-month contract, and she couldn't wait to go. She knew no one and I was worried for her, as she always had trouble making friends. Little did I know she was going to meet her own Disney prince while working there.

Another mail call my name was called, and I was handed a bulky manila envelope and instructed to stand by for inspection. I could see it was from my mother and was curious. I stood at the end of the line and watched as other women had their packages inspected. Not one to like surprises, I snuck a peek in the envelope and had a mild heart attack. Mama had sent me soft core porn. Well, mostly. It was the 2007 New York City Firefighters Calendar, except she only sent the pictures, with instructions to share with friends. They were quite mouthwatering, but I knew I was in deep shit. As the drill instructor passed each woman, I was mentally preparing myself for the ass-chewing, extra PT, and over-the-top outrage from the drill instructor. The closer she got, the worse the knots tightened.

As I handed the envelope to the drill instructor, she froze and stared past me. Behind me were the windows looking into the drill instructor hut, where they slept while on duty. The other side of the hut was a window that looked into our sister squad's bay. Our building was one long rectangle. We were on the bottom floor, and on the top floor were the platoons six weeks behind us in training. We called them our babies. Most days the blinds were closed, but on this day they were not. For a few seconds my drill instructor held my package, without looking at it. Then she yelled, "Turn to drill instructor square away time!" and rushed to the hut.

"Turn to drill instructor square away time, aye ma'am!" the women echoed. And I turned to see what had caused her to react: an all-out brawl on the other side. As the other recruits stared in disbelief, I ran to my footlocker and stuffed the photos to the bottom. Days later we found out what the brawl had been about. One recruit had gotten a letter and a photo from her boyfriend, who had recently graduated Parris Island. She was showing it off when another recruit snatched it from her. She had received the same letter and photo. They started shouting at each other, and one took a swing and had the unfortunate timing to strike the drill instructor, who had stepped in to break up the argument. As her fist connected with the sergeant's face, the instructor instinctively threw the recruit to the ground. The other recruits started shouting and swinging. It took six drill instructors to break up the brawl. For hours after lights out, I could still hear them outside being PTed in the sand pit.

CHAPTER 8

CINDERELLA SNAPPED

We had swim qualifications and drill practice, learned knife and bayonet skills, and fought each other with sticks that looked like giant Q-tips. We ran or marched everywhere and moved as one mass. Everything was synchronized. We stayed in 4th Battalion, on the other side of the island from the all-male battalions. Only twice did we not sleep in our own barracks: during the rifle range and during the Crucible. During the rifle range we slept in a barracks at the end of a long line filled with the men who were due to graduate with us. We saw them for two weeks as we learned to shoot and went back and forth from the chow hall. We were there for the Marine Corps Birthday and were rewarded with steak, lobster, and lots of cake.

One evening, as we marched back to our condemned barracks, we noticed that the men in the barracks we were passing had not covered their windows. Our drill instructor was calling cadence and randomly calling out drill commands. One required us to pivot slightly and march diagonally from the direction we had been marching. She called it, and not a single recruit obeyed the command. We were too busy watching the men. They were getting ready for showers, and we could see that all seventy of them were naked. They were standing in front of the racks, on the line, yelling "Aye, sir!" to their drill instructor before being released to shower. We showered the same way, all naked and standing in a line that passed beneath several shower heads. The line moved quickly, and you had only about thirty seconds to soap up and rinse off. It was no wonder everyone stunk to high heaven.

The rifle range was the first time I ever had a hallucination due to sleep deprivation. It was around two in the morning, and I was on duty. We rotated duty so that two recruits were awake to watch over the platoon. We did regular bed checks and did the laundry, refilled canteens, and checked gear. Which was worse? Getting up in the middle of the night for your shift or having to get up two hours early? I preferred the first shift of the night.

We needed to make sure no one was trying to escape or causing trouble. I was between the last occupied bunks and the empty ones when, out of the corner of my eye, I saw a recruit walk past me toward the back door. I turned around and jumped out from the racks to stop her, but there was no one there. I asked the other recruit on duty if she had seen her, and she had not. We did a count, and every recruit was in her rack. She whispered that I had seen a ghost, and that there was a cemetery just across the street that belonged to the family that had farmed the island before the Marines took control of it. I believed her and didn't sleep a wink when I got off duty. Today I know that hallucinations are a symptom of my mental illness, combined with stress, but that didn't get diagnosed until much later. But what is the difference between a hallucination, a vision, and a ghost?

We took classes on the history and customs of the Marine Corps, and I consistently scored higher than all others in my platoon. I was made the tutor, and in our little free time I tutored the women who were falling behind. Our platoon ended up getting the highest scores on the tests, beating out our sister platoon and all six of our brother platoons. We also beat them on the drill field. As a result, on the night before rifle qualifications, our drill instructors surprised us with pizza and a movie. We watched Enemy at the Gate, and the drill instructors paused it frequently to critique Ed Harris and Jude Law's shooting skills. We did not take first on the rifle range, but at least we were not last.

We learned the structure of the Marine Corps. There are three to four Marines in a fire team. Four to five fire teams in a squad. Three to four squads in a platoon. A group of platoons is a company, and a collection of companies is a battalion. The structure keeps going up and getting larger and larger, until you reach the Commandant of the Marine Corps. Just about each level of the structure had a headquarters on base, unless your direct supervising level was on the same base as you. A detachment is a subset of a battalion, and may or may not be at the same level as a company. On the aviation side of things, divisions become wings, battalions become groups, and companies become squadrons.

We learned the enlisted and officer ranks of both the Navy and the Marine Corps and had to easily identify them. In the fleet your ability to do this quickly hinged on how well you paid attention, and it was a steep learning curve. When outdoors the officers required salutes and the greeting of the day. The enlisted required initiating the greeting of the day, but only if they outranked you. You were required to state the rank of the person with your greeting, but only if they were enlisted. "Good morning, Sergeant Alvarez." It was a mouthful the higher the rank. "Good evening, Master Gunnery Sergeant Harris." Officers were to be greeted with "sir" or "ma'am." And you had better not call an enlisted person such, or you were guaranteed an ass chewing. The exception was drill instructors; they were also sirs and ma'ams. You were always to stand at parade rest for any Marine who outranked you.

The rule of thumb was, "If it's shiny, salute." Officer insignia were made of silver or gold, while enlisted insignia were matte black. But when you're on a base with Navy personnel you can forget about that rule, as the petty officer insignia is shiny silver. It was always fun to watch the "Is it? It isn't. No, it is" mental argument playing out in a new Marine's head as their arms jerk trying to decide if the petty officer is, in fact, an officer. Despite the name, a petty officer is an enlisted rank. Noncommissioned officers (NCOs) are also not officers.

My favorite part of boot camp was the obstacle course. My least favorite was the rappel tower. It was over fifty feet high, with six sides and a stairwell up the middle. The slow walk up those stairs made me weak in the knees. The higher I climbed, the more I felt like passing out. At the top I gripped the handrail so hard that my knuckles turned white. The recruit helping direct where to go whispered that he was afraid of heights as well, but this was all safe. I was called forward by a male drill instructor from 2nd Battalion. He got me in my harness and was giving me instructions on where to have my hands, one in front and one with my thumb up my ass. The Marine on the ground belaying me was my drill hat. I was shaking like a leaf, and I barely took notice of anyone else. My mouth was dry, and I wanted to lie down. I was instructed to stand facing the 2nd Battalion instructor and lean back. The top part of my body leaned, but the bottom half stayed standing straight. My legs would not budge. The drill instructor grabbed me by the front of my blouse, said, "Colby! Breathe!" and threw me off the tower. I fell about five feet and slammed into the side and hung there. The belay was working, and I wasn't going to fall. The rest was easy, and when I reached the ground, my legs were rubber.

 A week after Thanksgiving I had to have my wisdom teeth pulled. The Navy doctor did not have the same bedside manner as my dentist back home. I have never been a fan of dentists anyway and did my best not to think about the metal tools poking around my mouth. At home I would get laughing gas and headphones to drown out the drilling. Also, at home Mama would take me to Dairy Queen for a Blizzard after dental work, and we would laugh about me drooling until my mouth stopped being numb. This dentist visit was on a Thursday, Family Day, and the Marines set to graduate the next day were giving their loved ones a tour of base. There were families everywhere, and I cried. I missed my mother. The only upside of having major dental work done was that I got to sleep in the next day and have my soft food delivered to me, and I wasn't allowed to yell for three days.

 The last test of boot camp was the Crucible, a three-day field exercise in the wilderness. We used all the skills we had learned over the last three months. We crawled through mud, went on patrols, and slept in sleeping bags in aging huts with holes in them. They barely kept the December wind out, and several of the smaller women slept two to a bag for warmth. The wind cut right through you, and you felt as if you would never be warm again,

We were given two MREs to last the three days and had to ration. We went on night exercises and had to navigate the cold wilderness with just a compass and a map. Many groups got lost. Some of the time trucks with hot broth or hot chocolate came by, and we could warm up. I didn't care that my canteen cup had traces of mud in it; I was just so cold and hungry. The last thing we did was march fifteen kilometers back to our barracks. Parris Island isn't that big, so for a good portion of it we went in circles. Poor Dale was in pain, so I helped her along. As we hobbled together, I whispered Christmas songs to her. At the end of the march we were allowed showers and could finally get the mud out of our hair. A corpsman visited each of us, and I breathed low and slow to hide my nasty cough. I didn't want to risk being sent to medical and not being allowed to leave after graduation. Dale found out she had hairline fractures in her leg.

I struggled with my decision to join the Marines. The more classes we took on hand-to-hand combat, and the better I learned to shoot, the more nervous I got. I doubted I would ever be able to pull the trigger on another human being. I struggled with these things and often spoke about them with a chaplain. We debated the morality of war and whether God really would forgive someone who killed another person. Today these questions are still being debated as moral injury, an injury to the soul. I'm grateful that I never had to figure that out. My own moral injuries are about my not reporting abuse. My abusers went on to abuse other people, and I could have stopped them. How many people got hurt by my silence? Is their trauma my fault?

We graduated on December 20 and my parents, grandparents, and sisters came. I was surprised to see Guy had made the drive to South Carolina. They arrived the day before graduation and saw the Eagle, Globe, and Anchor ceremony, the moment we can officially call ourselves Marines. The Eagle, Globe, and Anchor is the symbol of the Marine Corps and is on every one of our uniforms. During the ceremony we're handed one made of brass, and it signifies that we can now call ourselves Marines. I saw Mama jumping up and down and tried not to cry as I was handed the cold bit of metal by Sergeant Martinez.

We got to spend that afternoon with our families, and I took pride in giving them a tour of the island. The next day was graduation, and as we were marching in and waiting at attention, Dad asked where I was. Guy said I was in the fifth platoon, second squad, third fire team. Dad still said he couldn't find me, and Guy repeated his words. Dad got frustrated and raised his voice: "I don't know what any of that means." There was a tense moment, as my family waited for Guy to explode. Out of character, Guy realized his error of "Marine speak" and told him I was in the fifth group of people, in the second line, second from the end. Mama breathed a sigh of relief.

After graduation we went back to the squad bay to gather my things. As we were walking back on the catwalk, I spotted a group of younger recruits marching in my direction. Mama suggested I move to the lower sidewalk, and I said, "No, watch this." Any time a platoon of recruits encountered a Marine or civilian who were not their drill instructors, they had to part the seas. Two squads would be on one side and two on the other, with the recruits facing away from the interloper, everyone yelling the greeting of the day. I knew what was going to happen and got sick joy out of it. Until I saw their drill instructor, and I instinctively came to attention. The sergeant stuck out her hand, looked me in the eye, and said, "Congratulations, Marine." The pride at hearing a stranger call me a Marine made my eyes well up, as I held back the tears and shook her hand as a peer.

We left the island, and I stayed with my family in their hotel on Hilton Head. It felt weird to sleep in a luxury bed after three months of a military-issued mattress. Normally Marines have only a week before having to report to their next training facility, but since it was so close to Christmas, we were given a month. I had to report to my recruiting station for recruiting assistance duty in a week.

The next morning we loaded the van with all my gear. I had two seabags and a garment bag, so Mama had told everyone to pack light. All the seats were taken, and any empty space was filled with luggage. Just before we left the hotel, I suggested making a head call, so my sister counted and said we were all here. I laughed and explained that a head was a bathroom. Somewhere along the way we stopped for gas, and I needed to relieve myself. I had just spent three months with women and had gotten used to our routines. When it was time for everyone to go to the head, we stood in line and did all we could to go as fast as possible. We women are not built for speed in this area. This included undoing our pants as we waited in line – anything to make the process go fast. As my sister and I made our way to the back of the gas station, I was on autopilot. Karen yelled, "Stesha Anne, what the hell are you doing?" I was undressing in the middle of the store.

For a former Girl Scout who loved the outdoors, Marine Combat Training was the best experience. We played with so many different weapons, and I was sad when I was not able to shoot the .50 cal. My arms were too short to reach anything, so I was passed over. In any case, I was going to be a linguist. My job would be in some dark bunker in the back of some base, behind walls of security. The Marines spend too much money on linguists to put us on the front line. Or so we were told.

My six weeks at Camp Geiger, North Carolina felt like a giant camping trip, except with live ammo and MREs. I learned to shoot grenade launchers and rocket launchers, and throw a live grenade. We did live fire exercises and learned to run while bullets were flying. We had to trust that the Marines behind the rifles would continue shooting straight. We became even more proficient in the M16 and were introduced to the M240 machine gun. We honed our skills at navigation, practiced tactical formations, and learned to recognize improvised explosive devices. We went on patrols, practiced martial arts, and watched real-world videos of interrogations.

We non-infantry personnel, or POGs – personnel other than grunts – knew we were just playing at it. The real stuff was taught at the Infantry Training Battalion on the other side of the camp. Occasionally we would get a glimpse of them through the trees, but we never interacted with them. Since every Marine must go through combat training, none of us could have a non-combatant job. No one could be a doctor, nurse, corpsman, or cleric. Since the Marine Corps is an offshoot of the Department of the Navy, these services were provided by the Navy. We knew the old saying that every Marine is a rifleman, but we also knew our statistical likelihood of being in the shit was not high. I would love to go back to that self-assured, limited way of viewing the world. We felt invincible; nothing could stop us.

After those blissfully fun six weeks, I was put on a plane to California. I was less than four weeks away from the incident that would be my undoing and lead to my decade-long struggle with substance abuse.

CHAPTER 9

COAST LINE

I'd like to tell you what an average day in the Marine Corps was like, but I can't. I was not an average Marine. There is no such thing. A Marine can do many different types of jobs, and each requires individualized training. Apart from medical and religious services, the Marine Corps is a self-sustaining institution. Marines can be truck drivers, mechanics, police officers, or fire fighters. They can be pilots, supply clerks, intelligence specialists, or reporters. They can be sanitation workers, cooks, payroll specialists, or infantry. Name a civilian job, and I can likely find you a corresponding

MOS (military occupational specialty). Some training is a month and some six; some jobs have a year or more of training. Some jobs only officers can do. Other jobs only enlisted can do. Every field and office has a combination of enlisted and officers working together to complete the mission.

Even at the DLI, the training time depended on your language. Spanish was the shortest at six months, Arabic and Chinese the longest at eighteen months. After DLI there was more training at Goodfellow Air Force Base, to learn the radio side of the linguist job. But not every Marine at DLI was a linguist. All active-duty graduates from the Navy and Marine Corps Intelligence Training Center in Dam Neck, Virginia were required to take the Defense Language Aptitude Battery (DLAB). If they passed, they were sent on to DLI. These Marines had the MOS designator of 0231, so we called them "oh twos." Other Marines had gone through a lateral move from a different MOS; still others were there on their second language. A few of the NCOs were reconnaissance Marines, and others were counterintelligence. But most of us were 26XX, or 26 hundreds. The XX code depended on your actual language, but you earned those upon passing the Defense Language Proficiency Test, or DLPT. We all feared the DLPT.

The first two and a half years of my enlistment were in a school environment. On top of that, the DLI was unlike any other training environment, and the Marines were permitted more freedoms than any other branch on the base. We could drive our own cars and have our families join us. We could drink and be loud and didn't have a curfew. Married Marines lived off post or in housing on neighboring Fort Ord. Ord had been used as a training base for soldiers during the 1940s, but it had long since closed. Most of the buildings were vacant and crumbling, but a good portion of the housing was still standing. By my second year I had friends who had gotten married to move out of the barracks, and weekend parties at their houses were common.

From the moment Marines got to DLI, we were given immediate

freedom. We could wear civilian clothes, leave the base, and drive cars. For the other branches it was not the same. The Navy had a thirty-day probationary curfew, and the Army had drill instructors and marched about for the first few months. The Air Force had the least freedom of any of us until their courses started. The Air Force treated them like babies, and so did we. We waited for them to get off the bus and asked what they got their badges for, tying their shoes? Marines are the cockiest bunch of assholes, and drunk Marines are even worse. But we do have the best-looking uniforms and the longest boot camp, so maybe there's a reason we're cocky. Marines at DLI are even cockier, because we had to make higher test scores on our DLAB. We had to score 110, while the others had to score 100. I scored 132.

The biggest freedom of all permitted to DLI Marines, not permissible in most other training environments, was that promotions were granted if you made the scores. The first promotions in the Marines are to private first class and lance corporal. These are at six months and nine months and are a given, so long as you don't get in bad trouble. Any higher promotions must be earned by your cutting scores, a combination of all of your quantifiable testing and time in service. This included scores from your PT test, rifle range, and swim qualifications. Notice that nowhere included is how good you are at your actual job. In every other MOS, or job field, promotions to corporal are done in the fleet. For whatever reason the training completion requirement was waived for DLI and, if your cutting scores were high enough, you could be promoted. The small flaw was that the scores were based on your MOS code. Given the part of the world where we were at war, the Arabic field had too many linguists in the higher ranks, so the necessary score was almost always unattainable. On the other hand, the Asian fields had fewer linguists in the high ranks, so their scores were almost always low. This caused a sour taste for most Arabic students, who felt they too should be promoted. In the field these training environment promotions are looked at with contempt, the consensus being that these Marines have not earned their stripes.

Still new to the Corps, I was concerned with my day-to-day life and trying to survive school. School had always come easy for me, but at DLI I learned quickly that the bare minimum would not cut it. I was attending class five days a week and for eight hours every day was not allowed to speak English. All too often words other than English would come out midsentence when I was in town, and you knew you had unconsciously switched based on the confused look from your friend. I began to dream in Arabic, and sometimes I would forget the English word for something.

DLI is on top of a small mountain, so if you wanted to go into town you had to walk down. The weather is not as sunny as you would expect, due to the combination of the cold ocean in the bay and the heat on the other side of the Santa Lucia mountains that cut Monterey off from the rest of California. As a result, there was almost always a fog over Monterey and our mountaintop. The fog is worse from late spring to early fall, due to the drastic difference in temperature. Once I took a picture of the bay from my window. The town and bay were covered in fog, but our mountaintop was clear. It was a sea of clouds from us to Santa Cruz.

I woke up at 5:00 a.m. to meet my platoon for physical training. If I was lucky, it would be in the base gym or calisthenics at the track further up from our barracks. If I was unlucky, it would be a beach run. Monterey is gorgeous early in the morning, but a forced run mars the beauty. I didn't mind running, but I hated having to keep up with the others. It didn't help that I was most often nursing a hangover. One such morning I still smelled like the bar, and Sergeant Miskelly groaned, "Please at least be twenty-one," before laying into me for falling behind. I hated that my inability to run fast was the reason my position of Fire Team Leader was taken away. Many leadership positions hinged on your physical abilities, rather than on your intellectual ones.

My least favorite of the beaches we ran was Asilomar, not because it was the furthest from our mountaintop base, but because in the early morning it always smelled like rotten fish and stale farts. I got faster at running, and by my second year I made the relay team. The eight fastest women were forced to join, and several times a year the team would compete against the other branches in front of everyone. I hated being required to join, because I knew I wasn't actually that fast, we just didn't have as many women in our unit as the other branches. There were fewer than forty of us. My one and only meet was on one of the worst days of the 2008 Big Sur forest fire. The ash traveled the thirty miles from the forest and covered the field, but still we ran. Nothing short of lightning would keep Marines from PT.

After PT I would hit the showers, then skip breakfast in favor of a cigarette or two at the smoke pit. The thought of eating after working out turned my stomach, and the smoke pit gave me the chance to catch up with friends outside of my schoolhouse or class. You could always count on the lance corporal underground for the latest gossip. The head of the underground was always whoever was coming off duty, and they were usually kind enough to tell us who had gotten in trouble before hitting their own rack for some sleep. There were multiple smoke pits around the base, each for a different purpose. Before and after school was the pit in the parking lot behind our headquarters. During these hours it was rarely vacant. During school hours the old stage in the middle of the Arabic schoolhouses became our smoke pit, and you could compare notes and gripes without worrying that you were speaking English. When I wanted to be alone, late at night or on the weekends, it was the smoke pit on the berm above my barracks. On a fogless night you could see the bay between the trees, and it offered solitude.

While there I experienced my first earthquake. It was small, barely over a 3.0, and I barely noticed it. It was late at night and I was smoking at the pit on the berm, lost in thought. I was sitting on the picnic table, and my beer had fallen off. I was looking down at it, a little confused, when a Marine in his pajamas came running out of the barracks screaming, "Earthquake! We're having an earthquake!"

I could hear Brandy laughing hysterically on the other end of the line.

"That isn't even my funniest earthquake story," I told her. "That one involves Charlie's parents." Charlie is a man I would later date for three years. "There were a lot of earthquakes where he grew up. One night his mother felt the bed shake so hard she woke up. She ran through the house, waking up the boys, yelling '¡*Terremoto*!' She ran around for a few minutes before realizing nothing was shaking."

"If it wasn't an earthquake, why was the bed shaking?"

"Charlie's dad farted hard."

CHAPTER 10

100 BAD DAYS

My class was a group of twenty-four service members of various ranks and branches. Since the school wants you to be as comfortable as possible, rank was left at the door. We were assigned new names, usually closely related to your real name. I was "Samia," which means "from the heavens." We had six teachers, all native speakers and all immigrants. The teachers at DLI were all immigrants, many of them political refugees. There was a rumor that one of the Chinese teachers had been at Tiananmen Square.

Ustath was the word for a male teacher who taught higher education. *Ustatha* was a woman teacher. Two of my teachers were Sudanese and had escaped the ethnic cleansing of the war in Darfur. Another was Egyptian and had immigrated for work with his wife and their young child. Two of my teachers were Iraqi. One was Catholic and had to flee with her family in the middle of the night when her brother spoke out against a high-ranking political figure. The other had escaped during the Ramadan Revolution, which established the Ba'ath party. The final teacher was Kurdish and had fled his village during the Anfal Campaign. He was a university-educated man and had come back to his home village to teach English. He had written the first Kurdish-to-English dictionary, by hand. When he was a young boy, if you spoke Kurdish and wanted to learn English, you had to learn Modern Standard Arabic, or MSA, first. He wanted to change that.

Since all of the instructors were immigrants, most brought their families with them: parents, children, spouses, sometimes siblings. Some of the family members could get jobs on base or for the DOD, others couldn't. Many opened businesses in town. Monterey is a small town but has the most diverse food of any place I've lived or visited. You could get bibimbap, then go next door for pierogies. Sushi was across the street from a shawarma shop. The board game store was next door to a patisserie and down the street from a tea shop. Two of my favorite places in town were a Thai place where no one, and I do mean no one, on the staff spoke English, and an outdoor Indian hookah lounge that served the best jalfrezi in a walled garden, steps from Fisherman's Wharf.

My classmates were diverse. Some, like me, were new to the military. Others were NCOs, and a few were officers. Some had been recycled down from other courses, usually due to a serious illness or failing too many tests, but had potential if given enough time. We pushed some students down to lower classes. By the end, only eight remained. Two airmen hooked up and got pregnant. They both washed out early and married to stay together. Fletcher was an airman who was recycled to us. He was an arrogant punk from Fresno, and we were happy when he washed out. Michael was a Marine who later admitted to purposely failing just so he could get another MOS. We teased Seal that she should have joined the Navy instead of the Air Force. We were sad to see her go. I was also sad when Rachelle left. She was such a cool person, and Arabic was her third language. In the end it was me and another Marine called Edwards, two airmen, Cavi and Brundrett, and four soldiers: Savannah, Braak, Savannah's boyfriend, and a sergeant. He was the only one left who was not lower enlisted.

Arabic seems like a daunting language, given the alphabet and the guttural sounds. But the alphabet is easily learned. Almost every word can be broken down into a three-letter root word, which is usually a basic verb. Once memorized, the conjugation rules are straightforward and easier to learn than other languages. There are ten conjugation rules, such as regular, causative, and reciprocal.

Based on those rules you can change a root word, based on a specific set of letters, to a noun or a verb. Within the nouns there are letters to add to make it a place, a person, or the active participle (the doer). Within the verbs, the letters added could make it past or present, active or passive. It's all very mathematical. For example, *darasa* is "to study," while *adrus* is "I study." *Madrasa* (a place where you study) becomes school, while a lower education teacher (a person who causes study) is *mudaris*. If you can figure out the root word, you can generally figure out the meaning. Most of the dictionaries required you to break it down to the root. The problem with Arabic is not the conjugation rules, but that there are between 5,000 and 6,500 root words, to make over 12 million words.

After class I would study and drink, usually with others and almost always at Duffy's. In hindsight, drinking daily might not have been the best study plan. It loosened my tongue and made speaking the language easier, but when it came to reading and writing I suffered. There is a dark humor that every Marine is a borderline alcoholic. We took drinking to another level, and we reminded members of other branches that we were founded in a bar, so we had to uphold tradition. Your ability to be seen by your peers as a "good Marine" depended heavily on your ability to hold your alcohol. Nearly every good story or misadventure started with "I was at the bar." For us, those nights started at Duffy's.

Duffy's was a converted house just off the High Street gate. If you went out the Franklin Street gate, it was only a few blocks down the mountain then turn left on High Street, right next to the fence line. Erin, the bartender, loved us. We made her laugh, and she was protective of our group. Erin stood less than five feet tall and had a thick Australian accent. No one fucked with Erin. My favorite memory of her was the night I drank an airman under the table.

It was spaghetti night and I loved studying there, because it was usually quiet on Wednesdays. At this point in my career, I had slowed my drinking on weeknights. I would have a beer or two with dinner and study for my exams. I was a C student at best but tried as hard as I could. It is hard to take courses like economics and history when they're not in English. I was sitting at the bar, slowly drinking my beer and enjoying my spaghetti, when a new airman walked up and started making fun of me. He recognized that I was a Marine and was making comments like, "I thought Marines were drinkers, and you're nursing your beer? What are you, a pussy?"

Before I could slug the idiot, Erin stepped in. "I bet you that she can drink you under the table. If she outdrinks you, you pay both tabs. If you outdrink her, I'll cover both tabs." The anxious airman let me finish my dinner before the drinking started. By the end of the night he was out a couple hundred dollars, and the next morning I regretted my hangover. We had a platoon run, and I kept falling out. One of the NCOs joked that I smelled like a bar. But hey, I won.

The other bar that tolerated our antics was the Legion, at the other end of High Street, to the right when walking down from the Franklin gate, on the way up to the campgrounds. The bottom floor of the Legion was the bar, pool hall, and karaoke setup. The second floor was the ballroom and kitchen. I went upstairs to the patio only a few times, but each time the view took my breath away.

The Legion was where we could be found most Saturday afternoons, as the beers were cheap and the liquor was poured strong. On one of those, after way too many drinks, I got the idea that I wanted to learn how to rock climb. I persuaded one of my drinking buddies to teach me, and it was the blind leading the blind. We went outside to the cliffside that soared above the Legion. My buddy instructed me where to put my feet and which rocks not to grab. I started off, with his nervous encouragement but without gear. "No, no, not that one. Yes, that's the one. Grab that one." When I fell, I felt like I had climbed a hundred feet. In reality, I fell only about five feet. I landed on my back and had the wind knocked out of me. I counted my lucky stars, but the bruises lasted a few days.

The other main gate was Prescott Street. Steps from the gate was Compagno's, a sandwich shop quite popular with all the branches. Bennett Compagno had been in the Navy and took over the shop from his dad. It was the only off-base place where a Marine could be seen in camis. Camis are a working uniform and not allowed to be worn off base, except when filling up gas on your way to or from work. The other uniforms, service and blues, are allowed off base because those are not working uniforms. Compagno's is small and crowded with shelves of chips, sodas, and beer. There's room for only two or three tables, so most people ate outside. During peak hours the line would be out the door and around the corner. The iconic sandwiches were huge and named after the different COs and NCOICs (Non-Commissioned Officers in Charge). The Mastery Guns Dobbs was a large hot sandwich with breaded chicken breast, lettuce, onions, and pickles, smothered in Caesar dressing. The unofficial "Marine Challenge" was to eat a whole Master Guns and a giant slice of cake and run a full PFT. If you didn't throw up, you won. I was never stupid or drunk enough to try that.

When you walk in, the store is covered in military memorabilia from service members who gifted Bennett with caps, photos, plaques, and unit t-shirts. Bennett is well loved, and service members would send him things years after leaving DLI. He understood that many of these young people were away from home for the first time, and he would do things to make them feel more at home. He would special order regional favorites from a student's hometown. In 2007 it was the only place in central California where you could get Big Red soda and Middleswarth potato chips. In 2021 I returned to Monterey and had lunch at Compagno's. It had not changed, except the names of the sandwiches. Bennett greeted me with a hug, and it was as if I were twenty-two again.

"I remember that Shawn made a special trip to Compagno's when he was on temporary duty in California. He went based on your suggestions." Shawn was a Kingsbury graduate who enlisted a few months before me. Shawn and Shannon were close friends with Paul. The two had gone in together with the buddy program, but Shannon washed out due to too many injuries. The final injury was when he fell from the Stairway to Heaven, a thirty-foot ladder-like tower on the obstacle course. He broke several ribs, and one pierced his lung. Combine that with twisting a knee on a run, and he was sent home. Shawn served out his contract and had an honorable discharge.

"What are Shawn and Shannon up to these days?"

"Shawn is doing well. As you know, he left active duty. He's running a business and chasing around kiddos. As for Shannon, who knows."

"When I was in college Shannon would blow up my phone, saying I needed to come live with him and be his live-in maid."

"Gross."

"I think he was living in Houston."

"Well, good riddance. What is it with you and these weirdos?"

I shrugged. "Who knows?"

I had met AJ on my first week at DLI. She took me under her wing, introduced me to all her friends, and gave me the ins and outs and dos and don'ts of the base. She seemed to have a lot of friends, and she had a cute boyfriend. I wanted to be like her. During my first full week there was an all hands "mandatory fun" day, a camaraderie-building event where the entire detachment was to be in the courtyard between the wings of the headquarters to have a barbecue. Our unit was small compared to the other branches. In 2007 there were about 200 Marines, 800 Navy, 5,000 Army, and 10,000 Air

Force. There were also a few hundred "others": foreign students, Coast Guard, Department of Defense, federal law enforcement, and "State Department," if you get my drift. If you looked hard enough, you could see these other students walking to class in their funny uniforms or civilian attire.

Since the Marine detachment was the smallest, we had only half of a U-shaped building that we shared with the Navy, and the courtyard was called "between the wings." We also had another full building up the hill, where all the women and some of the men lived. It was a typical California building, with an open-air stairwell in the middle and eight bedrooms on each side of three floors. Each of us had only one roommate, so it was more like college than any other base I had been on or would be on after. Later in the summer we were bunked three to a room.

This all-hands event was my first taste of what being in a real unit was like. All sorts of people mingling, cliques of friends and colleagues, laughter, lots of noise. I sat there with AJ as she alternated between being a social butterfly and paying attention to her boyfriend, Carra. AJ was about a year into her Arabic and belonged to 4th Platoon. Carra was a Korean student and belonged to 2nd Platoon. They seemed like a nice couple. I wanted to be their friend. AJ introduced me to all her friends, including a guy I would date for a few weeks. I felt included and I loved it. It wasn't until too late that I learned AJ was a backstabbing queen. She already had a reputation for being a liar and making up stories to get out of trouble. I didn't know how to read red flags. For the better part of my enlistment, I had difficulty with trusting the wrong people.

CHAPTER 11

Last Laugh

I had no idea why I was getting high fives from sailors in the chow hall. I was hung over and regretting having drunk so much the night before. But I was confused about the high fives. They continued for days, and my friends and I joked that I must have done something epically stupid. It was months before I found out what I had done, or rather what had been done to me.

I had been at DLI only a month or two when I met John. This particular afternoon, I was walking down Franklin Street and my goal was to have a few drinks at Duffy's, then venture into town and meet up with friends. There was no real plan. I was on the depressed side because I had been dumped by a guy I really liked. In hindsight the guy and I had only been on a few dates, but at twenty-two heartbreak is heartbreak. My friends were all his friends, and I wanted to have a moment to myself before I risked seeing him in town.

I was walking down, thinking about things, when my train of thought was disrupted by someone behind me, skating on those stupid shoes and calling my name.

"Hey, you're Colby, right?"

"Yes, and you are?" I had no idea who this short, skinny guy was. He didn't look even vaguely familiar, yet he knew exactly who I was.

"I'm John. I'm a Navy student in the Chinese schoolhouse." I still had no idea who he was, and I knew no Marines in the Chinese course, so I knew I hadn't been introduced to him.

"I'm sorry, I have no idea who you are. How do you know me?"

He laughed and explained that I wasn't supposed to know him. He had seen me in the chow hall and overheard my jokes about other branches. He admired how I could easily make my friends laugh. He also admired how the Marines always took over a section of the chow hall and everyone was too scared to go over there. It was a rite of passage to be invited to the Marines' table. I chuckled nervously and said I was sorry for insulting him. I hadn't realized other people were listening to what I was saying. John was not offended and began repeating silly jokes I had made like, "What do you call the Navy? A taxi service for the Marines." Or "What do ants and airmen have in common? One in ten thousand will fly." They weren't original, but they made people laugh. Many were rather colorful.

He asked if he could buy me a drink at Duffy's, and I gladly accepted. My non-plan of meeting up with friends didn't happen, as John bought me more and more drinks. We talked about why we had left college to join the service. We talked about stupid things we had done in the past and people we had dated. He told me he was a linguist because he had slept with an admiral's daughter and couldn't be a submariner. Apparently, the admiral was over the submarine fleet and refused to rubber stamp his schooling, so he chose a schoolhouse on the opposite coast.

Somewhere along the way I got completely trashed and began slurring my words, while John seemed to remain completely sober. He offered to walk me back up to base. That's where my memory ends. It was not uncommon for me to get blackout drunk if I didn't have anywhere to be the next morning, and I trusted that someone would get me back to base. Nor was it uncommon for me to wake up hung over in my own bunk, with no idea how I had gotten there. That next morning I did wake up in my own bunk, mad because my new jeans had a grass stain on them. I assumed I had fallen and scraped my knee.

What really happened is that John had walked me to my room, but first he made a short detour into the woods behind the line of barracks near the top of the hill. There was a walking path into the woods, a shortcut to the PX and Hilltop Track. My building was next door to a Navy barracks, and he chose to rape my unconscious body in full view of that building. Thirty sailors had seen him raping me, and no one had done anything to stop it. No one afterward thought to ask if I was okay or if I had been conscious. Instead, they gave me high fives. The stain in my jeans never did come out.

Sometimes images come in flashes, and I can picture lying in the dirt in the middle of the cold woods, but I don't know if they are real, or a figment from years of fixating on the rape.

The next guy I misplaced trust in was Alex Taylor. I met him late that summer. He was an "oh two" and came to DLI shortly before I did and was assigned to 4th Platoon like AJ. At this time the platoons were 1st (European and Euro-Asian languages), 2nd (non-Middle Eastern Asian languages), 3rd-5th (Arabic, grouped by schoolhouse 1, 2, or 3), and 6th (casuals). There was a big shakeup in the platoons shortly before I left, but this was how we were grouped for most of my time there. The three Middle Eastern schoolhouses had classes starting weekly, and there were at least one or two Marines in each class. A lot of us were learning Arabic.

Taylor's class picked up a few weeks before mine, so we studied together and were tutored by AJ. Over time I got my own tutor, and AJ began tutoring Taylor alone. He and I started dating around the time I found out about what John had done, and I just wanted to drink away the shame. The healthier option would have been to report John, but I didn't want my career to be over. Taylor didn't seem to notice that I was hurting and was always keen to get trashed.

The first few weeks it was fine. But I quickly tired of not remembering the next morning, and would tell Taylor I wanted to go back to the barracks after our date. Instead he would continue plying me with alcohol, and I would wake up in a hotel room he charged to me. I would throw up, then get mad at him and storm out. He would give me space for a day, then come to apologize, and I would forgive him. We repeated this cycle every payday, and each time I would be furious at him for violating my trust. I never remembered the sex because it was always after I got trashed beyond consciousness, but I surely remember the hangovers. To this day I cannot drink Corona without thinking of those lost months.

You would think I would have broken up with Taylor after the first or second time. Instead I continued forgiving him, then being mad at both him and myself when he again did exactly what he had promised not to do. I did dump him a few months later, when my parents were visiting. It was a Family Day, when family members and other civilians are invited to the Presidio to learn more about the different languages and cultures. There were pop-up kitchens, dancing, and cultural art shows. My class was too new to be involved, so we were supposed to watch and enjoy the time with our families. My parents had timed their trip to be there. They even planned to bring with them a young priest who had never been to California. I had reserved them a hotel room on base and met them at the gate. Taylor was supposed to meet us.

And did he ever, slurring his words before noon. After shaking my father's hand, he whipped out his penis and urinated on the tire of an officer's car. I ushered my parents and the priest away and promised them I would never go out with that guy again. And I didn't. But shaking him was not so easy.

A few weeks later Carra, AJ's boyfriend, came to find me, saying he couldn't find AJ. I was mad at her because she had taken Taylor's side in the breakup and had spread nasty rumors about me with the help of one of my roommates. I didn't care that Carra couldn't find her, and I told him so. He apologized and went on to look for her. Later that evening I found him at the smoke pit, crying and smoking, the contents of an entire pack of cigarettes at his feet. I felt sorry for him and asked what was wrong, and his tear-swollen eyes barely met mine. He had found AJ, and she was with Taylor.

"Okay, but they're always together. So, shouldn't you feel better?

Why are you crying?" I never did know what to do when I saw a man cry, and I've been known to be blunt.

"They're married." His shoulders slumped again. I had no idea what to do, so I offered him a menthol and a beer.

It turned out they had learned Taylor was failing and was going to be sent back to the intelligence community, and they wanted to stay together. Somewhere along the way their Arabic tutoring had become more of an anatomy and physiology lesson. If they got married, they would end up together when AJ graduated. Cool for them for getting their happily ever after, but that was a really fucked-up way to do it. I felt awful for Carra. I wish that was the last of them. By the early fall Taylor was gone, and AJ was mad he wasn't nearer. She took that out on me by loudly spreading the most vicious rumor yet: that I had raped Taylor after he told me he didn't want to go to a hotel room. Every time she saw me she would scream, "Rapist!" I could not get away from her fast enough. I thought everyone believed her, so I stopped hanging out with my friends in my platoon. No one bothered asking if everything was okay when they noticed a change in my behavior. No one thought to tell me they knew she was lying. I spent the next few months alone. It wasn't until years later that I learned no one believed her.

I entered what I call my first "ho phase." I loved dating and being with men. It was fun going out, and I loved the attention. One of my roommates took this as an opportunity to help AJ spread rumors about my sex life, some true but most lies. Apparently, I had slept with a lot more men than I was aware of. I felt it was my business who I spent time with and slept with.

CHAPTER 12

TWENTY-THREE

I met Aaron early in the fall of 2007. He was a Marine in the Korean schoolhouse, so we were not in the same platoon. I was in 3rd; he was in 2nd. Even though our base was small, the platoons rarely interacted with each other. They were like close-knit, competitive families. I didn't feel at home in my platoon, and after that summer I had few friends I could actually call mine.

I had finally been placed on remedial PT, not because I couldn't pass, but because I was overweight. The Marines are quite strict about their weight standards, so strict that the standards hadn't been changed since the 1990s and did not take into consideration the variety of body types. I was five foot two and between 145 and 150 pounds, considered fat by the body standards. Sure, I ate mostly the junk food offered at the chow hall. I also had a sweet tooth. But that alone was not enough to make me fail weight standards. My failure was because of my body. I am short and stocky, with a large gift at the front and almost nothing in the rear.

I showed up on my first workout to find myself surrounded by other Marines who did not look like they should be on remedial PT either. Aaron was like me: short and stocky. The Marines don't know what to do with people like us, so they set out to destroy us with extra PT and stress and thoughts of losing our jobs. It was a cold and rainy morning, and we were told to "just run three miles." To make sure we did it, we were each paired with another Marine. I don't remember why they paired me with Aaron, but I'm glad they did. He became a huge part of my life for the rest of my time in Monterey.

The three miles were not timed, so it didn't matter how fast we ran. Aaron helped me kill time on that slow and exhausting morning. We would talk for three-quarters of the track, then sprint the leg in front of the NCOs. I was probably hung over. Aaron got me to open up about my life, and he opened up about his. In that moment I started falling in love with him, but I had a boyfriend. Trey and I were not overly serious, but we were committed. I was looking forward to his visit the next month. He was an infantryman I had met that summer. I had borrowed a car and driven down to Camp Pendleton to hang out with an old buddy. At the last minute my friend was put on duty and asked one of his platoonmates to show me around. Trey and I hit it off immediately and had a fun time. We drove down to San Diego and rented a hotel room on Coronado Island. In the morning we watched the SEALs running on the beach and were happy to not be at PT ourselves. We toured the USS Midway and were sad when I had to return to Monterey.

I visited a few more times over the next few months and, to save money, Trey would sneak me into his barracks room. On one of those visits I woke with a start to hear a voice outside screaming, "Form up, Third!" I was in 3rd Platoon. For a second I forgot where I was and started scrambling to get clothes on. Trey told me to ignore it and come back to bed. I peeked out the window to see a Marine naked, except for combat boots, marching back and forth in the parking lot with the 3rd Platoon guidon. "He does this when he's really drunk," said Trey. "Now let's go back to sleep."

Over the next few weeks I got to know Aaron and his friends more, especially his best friend Ron. They were good men. I fell into their group as if we had known each other for years. We played darts at Duffy's, had late-night Waffle House meetups to sober up, and camped out on the beach on weekends if we didn't want to go back to base. There was an alcove a few miles up the shore from the pier, and most of the cops didn't care that parties were thrown there. But Trey remained in the back of my mind. I was falling in love with Aaron and needed to break up with the guy. He deserved that. But the question was how. Trey came to visit the week before our Marine Corps Ball in November 2007. Ideally he would have been my date to the ball, but his ball was the same weekend. We each were required to attend our own ball, so he had wanted to come up the weekend before. Note to self: If you want to remain friends with an ex, don't have him drive six hours and then break up with him on the first day.

I told Aaron that Trey and I were through and suggested we go to the ball together, as friends. He saw straight through that and asked me out. There was just one problem that prevented us from being able to date openly: He was married. The Marines definitely frown on adultery, but we justified it by telling ourselves he wasn't really married. His so-called wife had disappeared on him while he was in boot camp, and he had no idea where to send the divorce papers. He tried for another year to find her, and a private investigator finally tracked her down outside Vegas.

My relationship with Aaron was loving, but not healthy. We both drank too much, and we fought like crazy. I was in the middle of a mental health crisis and was self-medicating with alcohol, in lieu of risking ruining my career by asking for help. As a result, I could be an absolute bitch and would pick fights with Aaron and accuse him of cheating. I would get drunk and blow up his phone if he didn't respond right away. Other times I would be kind and thoughtful. It probably gave him whiplash, never knowing which side of me was going to show up. I never understood why he stayed with me. I never understood why he loved me. He never called me "psycho" or "bitch." For some reason, Aaron was keen to keep up with my crazy.

✽

Monterey was two of the toughest years of my life. I studied Arabic from sunup to sundown and attended classes like economics and religious history, taught in a language I barely understood. It was odd to be among peers, every one of whom was the smartest kid in the room. I exercised myself into physical injuries and am still paying the price. I stood tall against giants and shrank under the stress of untreated mental illness. I cracked under pressure about once a weekend, but each Monday morning I woke up, ready to take it all on again.

Monterey was also the best two years of my life. I did incredibly fun and stupidly reckless things. I had an amazing partner I loved deeply. I lived through events that could and should have killed me. I played softball with an ocean view, ate food ordered for me in languages I didn't speak, and fell asleep with the chatter of Monterey seals coming through the open window. To me the weather was perfect; I liked dreary fog. I hiked all over the peninsula, usually by myself, thinking about things. Some of this book was written from those long hikes.

CHAPTER 13

HOTEL WALLS

Prior to the pandemic, it was not normal for a twenty-three-year-old to come down with pneumonia. It was certainly not normal for someone so young to have it for a month and a half. I was so sick that a person could hear the rattle in my lungs from across the room.

Did I pause going to class? Did I go to the hospital? Did I ask for a sick day? Did I stop smoking? Absolutely not. Each day I would go down to the base medical, submit myself for more testing, then go to class. I saw this as a sign of my "badassness," a badge of honor, rather than as a mark of stubborn stupidity. I was not allowed to do PT with my platoon, so I begged for a "PT at own pace" chit and worked out in the afternoon with a friend. I hoped I wasn't contagious, but I gave it to Aaron. I can't remember exactly when I got sick, but I remember it happening shortly after we got back from a skiing trip to Tahoe; or maybe it was because of Tahoe.

Four weeks later I was still sick, and not enjoying Valentine's Day very much. Aaron and I had scraped together enough to rent a hotel room downtown. Our plan was to have a fun, sexy holiday and take a break from reality. Instead we were both sick, and we had to attend an all-

hands PT test thrown together by an angry little man who was furious that his wife had asked for a divorce. The sick ones usually are not forced to take PT tests, but are required to show up. Aaron and I showed up, as required, and went to stand with the sick bodies when the gunnery sergeant, or gunny, started screaming at us to get ready to run. My NCO, Sergeant Phillips, went ballistic. The other NCOs who knew how ill I was got in the gunny's face and demanded that he reconsider making me run three miles. He didn't back down, yelling that I had a "PT at own pace" chit and, by definition, a three-mile timed PT run was "at own pace," so I should run it with everyone else.

I panicked. I had barely gotten off remedial PT due to my weight, and the first class Physical Fitness Test (PFT) was the only thing keeping me from going back on the program. I was allowed an extra four percent body fat, and I knew this run would not be up to par. I dreaded failing it, because I had promised myself that if I lost weight to join the Marines, I would never let myself get put in the remedial program. It's a "three strikes and you're out" sort of deal, and I already had one strike. I could not afford to join it again so early in my career.

Sergeant Phillips stomped over to me, redder than I had ever seen him, and explained between gritted teeth that I had to run three miles. He ordered me not to push myself and said, "I don't care if you fail. Just don't die." I felt like I had an elephant sitting on my lungs, and the humidity of the seaside air didn't help. I took slow, shallow breaths to keep from choking and started off. One foot in front of the other. If I could make it to the halfway mark in under fourteen minutes, I could turn around and make it back in twenty-eight, with two minutes to spare before I was considered failing. My usual times were not much faster, usually around twenty-four minutes. I just couldn't fail. Every footfall I told myself, "Just one more step." One more and one more and one more.

Every breath was pure agony, but I stifled the cough. If I started coughing, I wouldn't be able to stop. If I couldn't stop coughing, I would throw up. If I threw up, I would fall out and fail. I just couldn't fail. I made it to the halfway point in sixteen minutes. Great. Now I had to try to shuffle faster for the second leg. So I picked people ahead of me and passed them. Every Marine I passed felt like I had already won the race. I just had to pass more Marines. I felt bad for them, because I knew they were failing. Most, but not all, were also sick. I could see the line of trees that meant I had one mile to go. One more mile meant I wouldn't fail. One more mile meant I could go back to the hotel and sleep off the rest of the holiday weekend. I thought about how warm the room was and how comfortable the bed was. I thought about how Aaron made me feel safe and validated. I used that jolt of energy to pick up my feet faster.

I could see the trees, so I knew I was almost there. Just one more step. Just one more breath. My vision started to blur, and I couldn't breathe, but dammit, I was going to keep moving. I could hear people calling my name. I could feel people running with me. One mile to go, and my entire squad were now running beside me. My fire team leader was in front calling cadence. His best friend was on my left, telling me I was almost done. The rest of the guys were behind me, willing me forward. Sergeant Phillips was on my right, alternately yelling "Don't die!" and "She needs to be in the hospital, and she's passing you!"

I could hear nearly the entire detachment screaming my name. Marines I had never met before, Marines in other platoons, knew what a fucked-up deal I had gotten and empathized. My friends from other platoons lined the path and started running with me when I passed them. They had already run their three miles and were willingly running more out of solidarity. I couldn't feel my feet, but I could see them, and I could move forward. Two steps past the finish line I collapsed into the arms of our corpsman, who had oxygen at the ready. I threw up and blacked out but came to in time to see Sergeant Phillips in a screaming match with the angry gunny. I caught bits and pieces, words like "psycho," "just go get laid," and "go to hell" being thrown around. I saw other NCOs backing mine, and I heard "insubordination" and "NJP" (non-judicial punishment) from the gunny. I laid my head on Aaron's shoulder and got high fives from my squad, because I had finished at 28.5 minutes. I had almost died, but I had not failed. The PFT ended up not counting, so I didn't lose my first-class scores. No one ended up being in trouble for insubordination. It was as if none of it had happened.

Somewhere during those six weeks of pneumonia, I met Private First Class Campbell, a new Marine assigned to my squad. She was in my fire team, which meant that as a lance corporal I was responsible for her, and her behavior reflected on me and my fire team as much as it did on our squad and platoon as a whole. My brain was basically mush after all the medications and weeks of being sick. One of the male Marines had gotten in trouble for partying with the local college students and had admitted to doing drugs. That meant that all two hundred-plus of us Marines had to take drug tests. We all had to line up in the hall and out the rear door of the U-shaped barracks building that doubled as the admin shop, into the courtyard that we shared with the Navy. Many Marines were bored to tears and were talking and laughing at the sailors as they headed to class. They had just switched to whites, and several Marines were yelling the bit from *A Few Good Men*.

Those with tests that day went first. Then the Marines who were in class. The casual status Marines went last. Campbell, being a new student, was with the rest of the casuals. This group was made up of brand-new Marines, those who had graduated and were waiting on going to Goodfellow Air Force Base for the second part of their training, and those who had been pulled from their classes and needed new orders. The ones awaiting new orders had either failed too many tests or gotten into trouble. This particular day there were quite a few troublemakers in casuals, and they were the ones making most of the jokes.

The detachment cadre were not pleased to be wasting a beautiful Monday morning handling the urine of grown adults, nor were they pleased that the jokesters were holding up the line. The staff sergeant running the show had already come out half a dozen times to tell everyone to shut up, pay attention, and keep the line moving. I had a class to get to and was about thirty minutes late. I didn't know if anyone had told our instructors, and my teacher, Ustatha Samira, did not like tardiness. I also did not know how I was going to tell her, in Arabic, why I was late. I was walking as fast as I could through the courtyard and had just come around the corner to where the end of the line was gathering. My schoolhouse was just across the street. I heard the staff sergeant yelling again, and I heard something else that stopped me in my tracks: PFC Campbell's voice, followed by laughter. She had decided to make fun of the staff sergeant before the door even closed, which meant that he had heard her.

I had a choice. I could let the staff NCO chew her out and run the risk of having a platoon punishment. Or I could chew her out myself. I turned on my heels and marched over to the unfortunate young woman. I was twenty-three, in decent-ish shape, struggling in school, sick, on the weaker side, and had a reputation as a quiet woman who had walls too high for most to get in. I had a few close friends but kept everyone else at arm's length. No one at the end of the line had ever heard me raise my voice. Until that day. The poor, unfortunate Marine was at parade rest and yelling "Aye, ma'am" to my questions, as if I were a drill instructor. The younger Marines were also at parade rest and the older Marines, the ones who had known me for a year and a half, were dumbfounded.

Should I have put the fear of God into a young Marine for making a joke? Probably not. But I definitely was not going to get in trouble for her blunder, when the person she was making fun of could have stripped both her and me of our ranks if he saw fit. Me giving her an ass chewing saved her ass, because I knew the other option was less pleasant.

Two events followed that made the day even more hilarious. After chewing out Campbell, I jogged to class and up the stairs. I was buzzing from the adrenaline of raising my voice and had forgotten the words I had memorized to explain why I, and the other

Marines, were late. I strung together a bunch of words from memory that I hoped made sense. The elderly Iraqi woman instantly blushed and was flustered. My classmates laughed nervously, and Savannah, sitting to my right, leaned over and whispered, "Why did you just tell us you had a bladder infection?" Turns out the Arabic words for "examination" and "infection" sound very similar, if you don't speak clearly.

The other funny moment was when Sergeant Phillips pulled me aside at lunch to ask me about the ass-chewing. I was confused, so he asked another way. On his third attempt he said, "Colby, why did you chew out PFC Campbell before you went to class?" I told him that it had happened weeks earlier, and that she deserved it for being disrespectful. He shook his head and reminded me that it had been that morning. When I looked frustrated, he put his hand on my shoulder and asked if my medications were making my brain fuzzy. I said yes. "Let me guess," he said. "It feels like someone has removed your brain and thrown it down the street, and you're trying to catch it." It was the most astute description of both mental illness and prescription drug interactions that I have ever heard.

The last few weeks of my bout with pneumonia were the hardest. I was on about ten medications, mostly to manage the side effects from the earlier medications. My doctors could not figure out why I wasn't getting better. By the end of my illness, I wasn't smoking or drinking, but I was still exercising. I did not want to be on the weight program again so soon after getting off it, but I wasn't resting as well as I should have been. I kept a plastic cup next to my bed so that if I got into a coughing fit, I could spit in it and breathe again. Aaron snuck into my room most nights because he was worried I would stop breathing in the middle of the night. My hands would shake trying to open a door or hold a phone, and I had difficulty comprehending texts.

I was weak from not eating. One of my antibiotics caused everything to taste like copper, and another made me forget how time worked. At one point Aaron asked me when I had last eaten, and I informed him I had had some of his pizza the night before.

"Stesha, that was Thursday! This is Sunday!" He made me force down some chow hall pasta, and all I wanted to do was throw it back up. Another time, a friend handed me a banana and said he was worried I was losing too much weight.

Every morning I would pretend I was fine. I would put on a smile and take my medications and down a cup or two of coffee. I prayed I would have enough energy to make it through the day, and at night I prayed I would wake up. In hindsight I belonged in the hospital, but I wanted to be tough and not admit weakness. Each night I would collapse in Aaron's arms and fall asleep, only to wake up to cough and spit.

Finally, the doctors had the idea to do an allergy panel, a last-ditch effort to figure out the source of the infection. Turns out I'm deathly allergic to three things that they tested for: two types of grass and cedars. Guess which type of grass grew year-round in Monterey's Mediterranean climate. A double dose of allergy medications and a shot, and my pneumonia began clearing up. The first Saturday night after my last round of medications, I decided to pull an all-nighter with Aaron and our friends. I was greeted with open arms by Erin and the staff at Duffy's. It didn't take me long to get toasted. Barely eating, dropping fifteen pounds, and not drinking for weeks had left me a lightweight.

After the fourth round, I thought I was invincible and stumbled outside for my first cigarette in a while. Halfway through, I started coughing so hard that I threw up in the planters that surrounded the small patio. Aaron held my hair back as always, and most of the others backed away. All except one young airman who wanted to add his two cents without ever having met me: "Um, should you be drinking and smoking if you're so sick?" I looked him dead in the eye and yelled, "Shut up, bitch, I'm Doc Fucking Holliday!" And I stormed back inside to ask Erin for some bread. Aaron couldn't help but laugh and shrug and repeat my words to the stunned airman. "You heard her. She's Doc Holliday." He then followed me back into the bar to make sure I didn't do something stupid, like fall off the bar stool.

CHAPTER 14

LADY LIKE

I loved my car. It was the perfect car for California, a baby blue eighties-era BMW, the boxy kind, with a sunroof. I had bought it from an officer for $400, and it never could pass inspection. I usually parked it on a side street instead of bringing it on base. I hated the automatic salute due to the blue sticker, so it was easier to park her off base until she got fixed up. She only lasted a year, but what a wonderful year it was. She was the reason I had freedom, but also the reason I was NJPed.

I had wanted a car and bought the first thing I could, never mind that I didn't know how to drive a stick shift. I was still learning to drive her when I stumbled upon Anthony. I could drive her around the base, and I could drive her around town, but she gave me lots of trouble driving up the mountain to the base. It was 9:00 p.m. and I needed cigarettes. The PX was closed, so I went to where I always went when I needed anything. Walking up to the smoke pit I saw a gaggle of young Marines killing time, putting off going to bed. I knew a few of them and emboldened myself: "Who here knows how to drive a stick shift?"

A few hands went up.

"Okay, and of you all, who would like to drive me and my car into town for smokes?" All hands went down. All except Anthony. I sort of knew Anthony from around the base and the off-base parties. I think he spoke Chinese. I had no reason not to trust him.

After we got in the car, he asked if I could buy him some vodka as payment. I didn't think twice and agreed. We went to the only liquor store that was open and sold cigarettes, then back to base and went our separate ways. I forgot about buying him the fifth of vodka until the next afternoon, when I saw it on the det gunny's desk. At midday I got a text from Sergeant Phillips: "Report to the det gunny after class." I knew better than to ask him, so I asked my fire team leader, Pisaruck. He claimed to have no idea, but I could see in his eyes that he was lying.

I didn't remember a word of what was taught that day, because I knew the other shoe was about to drop. My classmates all kept asking me what I had done, and I honestly could not remember. I went over the last few days and was drawing a blank. The only thing I could think of was that Aaron and I had been found out and were about to get court martialed for adultery. I texted him to see what he knew. Nada. Okay, so it wasn't that. If we were both going to be in trouble, then we both would have gotten a cryptic text. For the next five hours I kept playing it over and over and coming up empty.

When class was over, I dared not go up to my room first. I took my backpack and school things with me and headed to the gunny's office. I was trying not to shake when I knocked and said, "Lance Corporal Colby, reporting as ordered." I could hear him behind the door yelling into a phone, so I sat down in the chair next to his office and waited. I saw a friend who worked in the S1, the Admin shop, and asked him how much trouble I was in. "A lot," was all he said. Fuck! I still couldn't think what I had done.

When I was finally called in and saw the evidence of my crime sitting on the desk, empty except for an inch at the bottom, my heart sank. I had bought alcohol for an underage Marine and had been ratted out. The gunny could see it on my face. He asked all the questions, and I gave the correct answers. Lying would have made things worse. I tried not to cry when I heard the most dreaded words: "Non-judicial punishment," scheduled for Friday, along with Anthony and two other Marines. The gunny yelled at me for being so stupid, then his anger lost steam and he closed the door.

"Colby, be real with me. You're smarter than this."

"Yes, gunny. I know. I wasn't thinking."

"Well, no shit." He shook his head, and I was dismissed, free until Friday.

From several friends I pieced together what had happened. Anthony had downed most of the bottle before going to class. No one would have noticed anything except, by our luck, the Executive Officer decided to tour some of the Chinese schoolhouses and smelled the alcohol on Anthony the moment he walked in. It was also by our luck that he got one of the students to question him. Not just any student, but one of the counterintelligence students who was here on his second language. They told Anthony that if he didn't turn in the purchaser, they would have to review the security tapes from the shop and identify me. Poor kid stood no chance, and I really didn't blame him. But it didn't stop me from being mad in the moment. My of-age drinking buddies lambasted me for not lying to get out of trouble. I shrugged. I would never have liked myself if I had lied to save my job.

In the days leading up to the NJP, Aaron talked about what we would do if I lost my place in school. I was close to being finished, but that wouldn't save me. We'd seen guys closer to graduation being pulled and reclassified for less, and our CO had been throwing the book at underage drinking. He didn't know me from Adam, so why would he treat me any better? Leaving Aaron was going to hurt, but I figured I would survive it. Just so long as they didn't give me admin. Anything but admin.

Friday came and the platoons milled about between the wings. Some smiled in my direction, others attempted a thumbs-up in solidarity. I barely noticed any of them. The gunny told us what to expect. The CO would sit at the desk on the raised slab of concrete in the center of the courtyard. He would call us each, in order of rank, and read our charges. If we had someone speak on our behalf, they would speak next. The CO would then give his opinion on the crime, if he saw fit. He would then read our punishment and dismiss us.

Of the four being NJPed, I was the only one who could have been in trouble in a civilian court. Of the four, I was the highest ranking. I had been at the Presidio the longest. I had the most to lose. I stood next to the concrete podium, with its large oak desk brought in just for the occasion. I was facing my platoon, and I dared not catch anyone's eye for fear of crying. I told myself that in twenty or thirty minutes I would be on the other side of this. My bag was already packed, anticipating the temporary move to the restriction rooms.

A variety of punishments lay in front of me. The most obvious, reduction in rank, came with a reduction in pay. Two, half pay for up to two months. That would pack a hard punch if combined with the reduction in rank. Three, restriction for up to two months – a military grounding. I would go back and forth between my place of duty, school, and the restriction rooms. My babysitter on restriction would be the NCO on duty, and they often like to make life hell for restriction Marines, to make up for the fact that they can't sleep in their own bed and have to spend the weekend around a bunch of overgrown children. The unofficial punishment available was to be pulled from our schoolhouse to be reclassified. I could handle the others, as much as they might sting. But I was not ready to be separated from Aaron and my friends.

We were called to attention. Here we go.

The first Marine, Private Thomas, was called forward. He bumbled his salute and forgot to introduce himself. This was his second NJP in a matter of months, both for underage drinking. He never gave up who had given him the alcohol. Thank God it wasn't me. This time Thomas had been found by the officer on duty, half naked and passed out in the hallway. He had miscounted his floors and was pounding on the door of the wrong room. The women who lived there had been away. Thomas was already at the lowest rank possible. The CO laid into him for this being his second time in front of him. He had just gotten off restriction. No one spoke up for him. Half pay for two months, restriction for two months, and immediate withdrawal from the Arabic course. He forgot to properly dismiss himself and nearly fell down the stairs.

The second Marine, Private First Class Johnson, was called forward. She also messed up announcing herself and forgot to salute. The CO didn't even look up from his page. He read off her crime: forging the signature of an officer. She had been sick a few months prior and decided to make copies of her "Sick in Quarters" chit. This is a little piece of paper, signed by one of the base doctors, that we had to put on our door when we were sick. Johnson had been using them to get out of school and had gotten caught. If only she had actually been in her room when duty came calling, she might have gotten away with it. No one spoke up for her. Reduction in rank, half pay for two months, restriction for two months, and immediate withdrawal from the Arabic course. She started crying and ran off the stage without being dismissed.

Now Private First Class Anthony was called forward. My coconspirator. He too messed up his approach. I saw him out of the corner of my eye, and I felt bad for the glares he was getting from his own platoon. I've always felt bad that his platoonmates turned on him for turning me in. They saw his crime not as drinking but as ratting me out. They thought he should have taken his punishment "like a man" and not ruined another person's career. I saw him turning me in as an unfortunate error on my part. He also didn't have a single person speak up for him. Reduction in rank, half pay for two months, restriction for two months, and immediate withdrawal from the Chinese course. His voice shook as he dismissed himself.

My turn. "Lance Corporal Colby, report to the Commanding Officer." I felt my body move on autopilot. I pivoted, marched up the steps, pivoted again. I snapped to attention and saluted. "Lance

Corporal Colby, reporting as ordered!" I heard my voice as if coming from outside my body. I held my salute until I was told "at ease." I stood, at ease, in front of the man who held my career in his hands. I looked ahead and prayed it would be over soon. He read my crime and asked how I pleaded. Guilty as charged. He asked if anyone would be speaking up for me.

"Yes sir, Sergeant Phillips."

Sergeant Phillips was called forward and was quickly at my side, saluting. I heard him call me a mediocre student but one who tried harder than anyone else in my squad. He had known me for over a year and had seen me struggle daily, but I always had a good head on my shoulders. This error of judgement was a fluke. Sergeant Phillips was dismissed, and it was time for my punishment. Reduction in rank. Half pay for two months, suspended. Restriction for two months, suspended. And then it was over. I was dismissed and confused. That was it? What did it mean? Where was the rest? Had I heard him wrong? I saluted and dismissed myself, properly and without tears. The detachment was released and free to start their Friday. We four went to the det gunny's office to await further instructions.

The first thing that had to be done was to remove our ranks. I put on one of the sets of PFC chevrons. Then the other three needed to gather their things and report to the duty NCO for restriction. That left me in the office, and I bluntly asked the gunny to explain what I needed to do. The CO's words hadn't yet fully sunk in. Could I really have gotten off so easy, when the others had had the book thrown at them? What did my punishment even mean? A suspended punishment meant that if I got in trouble again during the next six months, the previous punishments would be enacted, plus whatever new punishment I received.

The gunny closed his door for the second time that week and explained why I had gotten off easier than the others.

The CO, having inherited an alcoholic unit, had wanted to come down hard on me. In his first few weeks there had been several dozen NJPs at once, and the restriction rooms had just cleared. It was our super scary and aloof XO who had come to my defense, along with the gunny and the first sergeant. I didn't know that the first sergeant and the XO even knew my name, much less knew me well enough to defend me. They told the CO that throwing the book at me would be incredibly unfair, as I was a good Marine who kept her head down. I threw my whole self into everything, and they saw it. I had made a mistake that was out of character.

I thanked the gunny, and he looked me in the eye. "Don't make a liar out of me, Colby." I nodded and promised I wouldn't and left the office, ready to change and meet up with Aaron. We met at the smoke pit in our civis and planned out the weekend. While we were smoking, a Marine I knew only in passing ran over and started yelling at me. "Colby, what the fuck do you think you're doing? You're on restriction! You shouldn't get caught out here. You're making a huge mistake."

I looked at him, dumbfounded. "Dude, did you not actually listen? It was all suspended, except for the reduction in rank."

He blinked. "Oh, I wasn't actually listening by the time it was your turn."

I couldn't help but laugh. It was that way for the next few days, especially when I showed up at the beach bonfire that weekend. Of course, I left immediately when I saw how many underage Marines were there with beers in their hands. No one had actually learned a lesson from that embarrassing display of power by the CO. Over the next few weeks I heard the whispers, and once I overheard a few junior Marines explain to a NUG (new useless guy) how I had faced my punishment in the most badass way possible, with nerves of steel. Didn't he know how badly I was shaking inside?

"Can we take a moment to talk about how stupid it is that he was 'underage'"? Brandy was clearly flabbergasted. I was getting a little anxious and was pacing around the kitchen island. Telling the story about my NJP always made me a bit mad. I poured myself a drink. "It makes it sound like you gave alcohol to a fifteen-year-old!"

"I know. Mama always would tell me that if you were in the military, you should be allowed to drink at any age. It's okay to take a bullet for your country at eighteen, but heaven forbid you have a beer with your buddies."

"It just makes zero sense."

"Brandy, you're preaching to the choir."

CHAPTER 15

Memory Lane

What I learned from my NJP was that I had to choose my friends more wisely, so I shut a lot of people out. I brought my inner circle down to three or four. I tested people out to see if they belonged in my circle. One who passed the test was Vaughn, who became like a little brother to me. He was a great addition, even though he was underage. No alcohol for him! I knew Aaron would like him, too. I also was looking forward to meeting his girlfriend. She was supposed to drive out from Oklahoma in a few weeks for the ball.

When other Marines in the common room asked Vaughn what he had been up to, he replied, "Oh, I made a new friend. She's pretty cool." He let my name slip and was interrupted by Philip Winkler, who had been watching TV. "You're mistaken," he said. "Colby isn't good friends with anyone. She has walls, that one." When Vaughn repeated the conversation to me, I felt both hurt and proud. I had thought Winkler was my friend and was hurt that he thought otherwise. But I was proud that others saw me as unapproachable. Unapproachable makes it harder to get hurt. Unapproachable makes it easier to leave when things get too crazy. Unapproachable also makes it easier to get left behind.

One Saturday, Vaughn and I were on our way to San Jose, one of the few cities outside Monterey that we could go to without permission. San Francisco required either a four-day weekend or prior permission. I hated asking permission for anything. We were headed to San Jose to get a part for my car. The speedometer had stopped working, and I was just guesstimating my speed based on the odometer. Probably not the best idea, but oh well. Vaughn had fallen asleep, but I didn't mind. The hills and mountains between Monterey and San Jose make for a gorgeous drive, so I was pleased to have a little time when my head could just wander. I was smoking, of course, and the ashtray was a bit too full. I did the horrible thing and threw my cigarette out the window.

I kept letting my mind wander while I drove. About five minutes later I smelled smoke and saw a small fire in Vaughn's lap. My cigarette had come back though the open sunroof. I was on an incline with no shoulder, so I had to put it out now! I reached over and slapped Vaughn's crotch. Well, that woke him up. I yelled "Fire!" and he put out the small flame. Sadly, there was a small burn hole in his brand-new jacket. He started laughing and replied that no one was going to mistake his jacket for theirs anymore. I still feel bad, because it was an expensive jacket for a private.

October 2008 was a lonely month for me. Aaron's class was on a month-long immersion trip to Korea, and I was able to talk to him only once over the satellite phone. It felt weird hanging out with the guys without him, and I realized that I had few friends who were one hundred percent mine. I liked being on my own from time to time, but a whole month was depressing. But about halfway through the month I met Vaughn, and it was nice to be able to hang out with someone new.

I made one other friend while Aaron was away. It was Halloween, and Aaron was due back from Korea the next morning. A friend and I decided to go as Bonnie and Clyde, mainly so I could wear this little black dress and a cute hat I had found at Target. Clyde was a Korean student and a friend of mine and Aaron's. He did not disappoint in his three-piece suit. Our first stop was, of course, Duffy's. By our second stop at the Crown and Anchor, Clyde ditched me to chase after a woman, and I was on my own.

The Crown and Anchor was not my usual hangout due to how big it is. It's in the middle of Monterey's downtown and popular with civilians and military alike. It was more packed than I had ever seen it. It was wall-to-wall people and, at five foot two, I was having trouble getting the bartender's attention. After a few failed attempts, I was considering calling it a night. That is, until I heard a voice from behind me: "What are you having?" I turned and had to look up into a very tall pair of bright blue eyes. He flagged down the bartender and gave him our order.

I recognized him from one of the other platoons, but I couldn't recall his name. I was embarrassed because he knew mine. I'm always embarrassed when a person knows me and I don't know them. His name was Lucas, Luke for short, and he was a Russian student. I laughed at the irony and told him that Russian had been my original choice, but HQ at the time were letting in Russian students only every twelve months. I had missed the previous class by a few months and wasn't going to be allowed to remain in casual status for nine months when there were spots in the Arabic schoolhouse picking up weekly. The Cold War was over, after all, and Russian linguists were not a priority.

Luke told me how he already spoke Russian, having served as a Mormon missionary, so he was all but guaranteed a spot. Cue my joke about a bar being the last place I expected to find a former missionary. He told me about his lapse in faith, and I told him about my mistrust of Mormons. Pretty heavy bar talk for a crowded Halloween night. People are partying around us, and we're chatting about religion and trauma. He teased me on my girly drinks, and I nearly choked when I took a sip of his Wild Turkey.

Luke and I talked all night, bar hopping through downtown. After the bars closed we ended up at a pizza joint known for staying open late. The cab service in town stayed busy and you had to wait quite a while, especially on a night like this. At the pizza place we ran into Clyde and his new lady friend, and he apologized profusely for leaving me behind. I teased him about never leaving a Marine behind but didn't actually care. My night had turned out pretty cool, and I had made a new friend. After pizza had soaked up some of our buzz, we decided to walk back up Franklin Street to the base. It's only a mile, but uphill the whole way. A little difficult to do both drunk and in heels, so we went slow. At one point I gave up on the heels and chose to walk barefoot on the sidewalk. Luke held my shoes. He walked me to my barracks, then went on further up the hill to his own.

Luke was the kind of guy you could trust implicitly. He was kind and thoughtful. He was the kind of guy who would buy you a steak dinner if he found out you were hungry and money was tight. He was a musician and had played the upright bass in college. He played various other musical instruments. My favorite photo of him is with his guitar, in his camis, slouched against the wall of the barrack catwalk.

When Aaron returned on November 1, he also agreed that Vaughn was a cool kid. He was pleased I had made new friends. We invited Vaughn and Luke to hang out with us. Vaughn went to Southern California with us for Thanksgiving and was our designated driver for my birthday. We took another friend, Stephanie, with us. Neither could afford to go home, and we didn't want them to eat dry chow hall turkey. I was driving through Bakersfield as everyone else slept. The smell woke Stephanie up, thinking someone had terrible gas. She rolled down the window, thinking it would get better.

"Oh God, the smell is outside? I can taste it! Why does it smell like rotting cabbage farts?!" She obviously had never been to Bakersfield.

Vaughn shared a suite with us for the ball, and he was accepted by our other friends. He really was like a little brother. I regret not keeping in better touch with him after I left DLI. Luke and I did keep in touch. The last time I saw him was at my going-away party in February 2009. He showed up at Duffy's with all our other friends, wishing me well on my next adventure. We kept in touch for many years by text message and phone calls and Facebook.

CHAPTER 16

SOMEBODY I USED TO KNOW

It always seemed that when the detachment was bored, or in a lot of trouble, they would shake up the room assignments. In my two years at the Presidio, I had five permanent roommates. My last room assignment was solo, with the S4, the supply shop, having the option to give me a temporary roommate for a few nights when a new female arrived on the base. That was my favorite room. It was twice the size of a normal room, so I pushed all the furniture to one side and bunked the beds. Aaron brought up his Guitar Hero, and my room was where the gaming sessions took place each night. And since I didn't have a permanent roommate, I was allowed to have beer. Everyone knew I had it, but they also knew I was not going to give any to any underage Marines.

Of the five roomies my favorite was Soda, and she was also the longest. We roomed together for almost a year. Soda wasn't her real last name; that was Sakoda-Chang. She was the shortest person in the detachment, barely tall enough to enter the Corps. She was from Hawaii and complained that the water in the bay was too cold to do what the locals called surfing. She would laugh at the tiny waves and talk about the real waves on her home island.

Soda entered the Arabic course shortly after I did, but her class had already surpassed mine and was able to go on an immersion trip. The top ten students from each language were given the opportunity to study for a month in a country of their language. Hers was Egypt and mine was Jordan, though I was ranked number eleven. I prayed one of the others would get sick so I could go, but that didn't happen. I still have the hand-painted prayer beads Soda brought back for me.

We laughed about her assignment because they were not allowed to tell anyone they were American, and they definitely couldn't tell anyone they were American servicemembers. They were also not allowed to speak English. They were supposed to blend in. "Oh, yeah, we don't scream 'Americans' everywhere we go," Soda laughed. Her assigned partner was a six-foot-tall redhead from Oklahoma.

My worst roommate was Avery. The command wanted to try something new and have everyone three to a room. That didn't last long. Avery had been with me since boot camp, and I despised her for the sheer fact that she reminded me of everything I hated about myself. She failed the PFT and was on remedial PT. She was also on restriction for skipping the remedial PT and lying about it to her squad leader. As a result, I had to go with her to the early morning PT to ensure she was going. I was rewarded by being allowed to skip my platoon's regular afternoon PT, but I still hated having to get up that early in the morning. Our other roommate Snider and I would take turns on "Avery duty."

We would get back from PT, and I would take the first shower. Instead of waiting to take a shower after me, Avery would get dressed for breakfast and formation. We were required to wear a green t-shirt and green shorts under our camis, referred to as green-on-green, and she would just wear the same ones she had exercised in. Nor would she change her sports bra or underwear. After class restriction Marines would report to the duty NCO for their assignments, usually cleaning the head or whatever else the NCO wanted them to do. Normally a Marine on restriction would sleep in a different room nearer the duty hut, but all were filled with males, so Avery was allowed to stay in our room.

Restriction Marines were required to stay in their camis after class, while the rest of us were allowed to change into civilian clothes. She would come back to our room and drop her camis on the floor and sleep in the same green-on-green she had been wearing all day. The next day was the same thing. The spot on the floor where she would drop her camis had a permanent grease stain. She was finally ordered to shower and wash her clothes when people started to complain about the smell. As her roommates, we were responsible for supervising this as well.

Late one Friday night I was returning to the barracks, drunk off my ass. When I opened the exterior door to our deck, I could smell our room. It was at the end of the short hallway, and with each step I became more and more disgusted and furious. I reached our door, and it took me a few tries to get the key card to work, the entire time swearing out loud about how much I hated being stuck with her. I finally got the door open and saw that Snider and her boyfriend Coats were on her bed watching a movie. Snider's bed was to the right of our door, and the suite bathroom was to the left. My and Avery's bunks were past the bathroom. I had drawn the short straw as to who had to share a bunk with her, and my bed was on the bottom bunk.

I swayed as I grabbed the Lysol and air spray that held a permanent place on Snider's bedside table, stumbled to my bunk, still swearing, and sprayed Avery's bed, with one can in each hand. I stumbled back to Snider's table. Snider and Coats were roaring with laughter, holding their sides. Snider managed to choke out "Avery is in her bed." I was too short to be able to see her. I went back to the bunk and passed out, without apologizing for spraying Avery in the face with Lysol.

Looking back on the months she was my roommate, I cringe. I didn't see how badly Avery was hurting, and the more she slipped into depression, the meaner I got. I yelled and screamed at her for nearly making us fail our room inspections. I hated her for telling AJ about the men I slept with, which helped give me a reputation for being easy. I saw it as my business who I slept with and none of hers. Definitely none of anyone else's. In hindsight, if I had been nicer to her, she might not have spread those rumors. I'm sorry for the way I treated her and wish I could apologize. She didn't last long in the Arabic course and ended up in Finance. I hope she had a wonderful career, away from the harsh intelligence community. If my book finds her, I hope it finds her well.

The Navy detachment ran things quite differently in their half of the building. For one, they were very particular about their smoke pit. There was a huge sign that said "Department of Navy Personnel Only." When I would join my friend Petty Officer Roberts for a smoke when he was on duty, sailors would yell at me to go away. Roberts would point to the sign and say, "The Marines are the Department of the Navy, so she gets to smoke here. Besides, I outrank you." I miss that guy, and I wish I could remember his first name and look him up. I'm actually not even certain his last name was Roberts.

Another thing that was different was that the Navy treated their side as if it were a boat. You had to salute and request permission to board. Occasionally, when our duty NCO was bored, he would send us over to the Navy side to cause trouble. Marines would go full reconnaissance and sneak in to steal toilet paper or cleaning supplies. It's no wonder the Navy hates us so much when we're deployed together. We would make fun of them and remind them that we're both naval units, and that there was no reason to act as if their barracks could take water any day now. They had a two-story anchor attached to their building. We joked that if Monterey flooded and it reached the base, it could be called to duty.

In November 2008, on the night of the ball, one of our platoons decided to paint their anchor pink. That would have been quite funny, except that the younger Marines took it too far. Some of them decided to tag multiple buildings, and they ruined the paint job of an eighties-era Russian tank that was the pride of the Russian schoolhouse. No one would have suspected anything, if one of the Marines hadn't tagged in his quite obscure language. That misstep caused his entire platoon to be punished for a month.

The people I remember most from my Marine Corps days are the artists. Many of them went on to have wonderful careers in the art world, and I'm always willing to drop some money when they sell their pieces. I remember going every Wednesday to open mic night in town to hear my friend Cooper play his guitar. His fingers moved along the strings, and his voice was perfect for the musical poetry. I still have his self-recorded EP and can sing the words to my favorite song, "Feathers." He wrote it about his future muse, as if she existed in his current reality. I went to tattoo parlors with my friends and admired the work of a Marine infantry veteran. Every one of his masterpieces was beautiful, and I'm proud to have one of them on my back. I took Vaughn to get one of his pieces, and many of my friends had work done by him. Sadly, he was fighting his own battles and was fired when he tried to set fire to the shop.

I admired these Marines for the versions of themselves they were sharing through their art. I cried over beers with many of them as they shared their demons, and I laughed at their jokes. The ones I admired most were the comedians, like Aaron who could get someone to laugh and shut down bullies with a quip.

My least favorite comedian was Wolfe. I liked the guy, but I found his rape and dead baby jokes in poor taste. But he sure got people laughing while we were waiting around between the wings. I never understood why grown adults were forced to stand around for the better part of an hour simply because their bosses didn't want them to be late. Everything was "fifteen minutes prior," and by the time it got down to the individual fire teams, we'd be standing around for an hour. Wolfe stood behind me in formation, and I was often forced to listen to his fantastical stories and tasteless jokes. Most of the time I kept my mouth shut, until the day I didn't.

Before I tell you what happened, I need to remind you a little of the geography of the base and about how we interacted with each other. The Air Force had most of the barracks on the base, and their "baby barracks" were the ones between the main gate and our detachment. The "baby girl barracks" were right across the street from us, and the joke was that if any male Marine needed a date for anything, especially the ball, he only had to walk into the building and announce himself, and he would have his pick. I found it was the same for female Marines. Men from other branches wanted to be my friend or bed me, just so they could say they knew a Marine. After John and Taylor, I got good at saying no to those who didn't deserve my attention. As I said, it's easy to be cocky when you wear an Eagle, Globe, and Anchor. On this particular day, Wolfe was trying to convince our platoonmates that he was going to go into the French Foreign Legion after leaving the Corps. In his mind, Legionnaires were more badass than Marines, and he wanted to always be the biggest and baddest guy on the block. He was telling some fanciful story about how the Legion had brothels full of prostitutes only for the Legionnaires' use. According to him it was a perfect setup because the women were not allowed to leave, so the Legionnaires didn't have to worry about secrets leaking that could hurt France. It sounded stupid and made up and a lot like human trafficking to me, and I was ready for him to change the subject or shut up. One of the guys next to him said, "Man, I wish the Marines had set up brothels for us! That would be awesome." Without turning around, I jumped in with, "They have. It's across the street." The stunned silence prior to the roaring laughter was perfect. No one expected quiet little me to say such a thing, and I basked in the back slaps and high fives.

CHAPTER 17

RUIN MY LIFE

The best sergeant I ever had was Sergeant Hank Phillips. The worst was Sergeant Randy Baker, whom I would meet later.

When Phillips came to DLI, we were both in casual status. He was a corporal, and most of the casuals were lower enlisted who were too scared to speak to him. Sure, he was an NCO, but that didn't mean he wasn't human. So I showed him where the chow hall was and told him a little about the base. I had been there a month longer, but NCOs were generally placed in a course more quickly than us lower enlisted. We got our placements at the same time, with courses starting a week apart. This put us in the same platoon. The day I took him to the chow hall, I got a glimpse into what the Marine Corps was really like. I also got a feel for what making a friend was like, if only the friend were not an NCO.

All the other casual Marines were years younger than me, but Corporal Phillips was closer to my age. He had seen the real shit in the infantry, before requesting a lateral move to be a linguist. He had been married, had been deployed, and had his ideas of what he would do if he were placed in command. From the beginning he took charge of the casual Marines and gained instant respect among them. Everyone just called him "Corporal," no last name. Any lower enlisted Marine knew exactly who you were talking about, as did all the Middle Eastern schoolhouses, or so it seemed. Everyone had their own "Corporal" stories glorifying his badassness, and I was proud that he was my squad leader. Everyone in his squad would have followed him to the gates of hell and back. We all wanted to be good Marines, if only to gain his approval.

I knew he thought of me as a decent enough Marine, because he used my rank with my last name. Marines he didn't like or approve of were referred to as "Mr." or "Ms." I had the honor of being referred to as Lance Corporal Colby. A year later, the worst thing about my public NJP was to hear him call me a "mediocre student" but worth taking a chance on. When he was promoted to sergeant everyone was confused, because they could no longer call him Corporal.

I ran into him once later in the civilian world. It was weird and surreal. I was attending the Student Veterans of America conference and had seen a few of the other Marines from DLI. I don't know why this shocked me. We had all separated around the same time, and it made sense for us to immediately use our GI Bill. But seeing faces I had known half a decade before was shocking. On my second full day Morris, one of the former Arabic students, informed me that Hank Phillips was there. "Just look for the biker dude with a ZZ Top beard," he said. Sure as shit, I spotted him on the escalator and turned around to bump into him. Five years had changed his appearance, but he was still my NCO. I loved seeing him. More recently he passed his licensing exams to become a marriage and family counselor.

DLI is where I started to change some of my beliefs. Prior to joining the Marines, I would have told you gay people were going to hell, because that is what I grew up hearing in the South. I heard adults say that being gay was unnatural and nasty and disgusting. I knew of a few people who got kicked out for being gay and I thought to myself that they deserved it.

Thankfully no one realized I held these beliefs, and one of my close friends came out to me. The "Don't Ask, Don't Tell" policy had not yet been repealed, so if you were found out to be gay you could be kicked out of the military. I sat quietly as we drove to San Jose and James told me about his boyfriend, who was a corpsman in North Carolina. They had been dating before they both went into the military, and keeping their relationship a secret from everyone was getting to be too much. I was honored that he trusted me but didn't know what to say. No one had ever come out to me before.

I had to have a come-to-Jesus session with myself: Did I really think James was going to hell? Did I think he should lose his job? He was a stellar Marine and spoke Arabic better than anyone I knew. Was it fair if he lost everything? To keep up his secret, he went on dates with women who looked like supermodels and laughed at the gay jokes Marines would tell. He was dying inside and could do nothing about it. I decided it wasn't my secret to tell, nor was I in a place to judge. Aaron and I were committing adultery and could also be in serious trouble if anyone with any weight behind their rank found out.

I must have appeared trustworthy, because several other Marines came out to me over the next few years. One told me he had been sexually assaulted by a sailor and was too terrified to report it for fear of being outed. He and the sailor had been seeing each other, and it was a case of date-rape. He couldn't say anything. Another Marine had been found out by his roommate and was being blackmailed. He also couldn't report any of it. I could not even imagine the stress these Marines were going through, and I came to hate the bigoted "Don't Ask, Don't Tell" law. None of these men were bad people, and none were bad at their jobs. Why should they risk losing their veterans benefits?

I know I was not the best student at DLI. I drank and partied more than I studied, and while studying I was usually drinking. I squeaked by with Cs, just enough to stay in class. While this strategy worked for passing the tests in the courses, it's no surprise that it didn't work for the final test: the DLPT. As it came closer and closer, our teachers began to panic. They were sure no one would pass. They often told us that our class was the lowest-performing class they had taught. During the first few months, classmates were pulled and reclassified if they couldn't meet various benchmarks. I took it as a good sign that I hadn't been reclassified yet. I had the misguided notion that I would do fine on the DLPT, since I did fine on other tests. I was wrong.

    A few months before it was time for our DLPT, we got word that it was changing. We were going to be taking the new DLPT 5. Rumors began to circulate that it was going to be harder than the four previous versions. We began to sweat. There was a meeting in the schoolhouse with the test designers and the most senior classes, the ones it was going to affect the most. We were told the first few classes would be the guinea pigs, and that if there were problems those would be fixed for the lower classes. The test designers introduced themselves, and I found it odd that one of them didn't speak Arabic. Her language was French.

    The closer to test day, the further I fell behind. We were no longer simply taking language classes. We had advanced far enough to take government, history, religion, and geography, all without a word in English. I understood just enough to get by, but it felt as if I understood none of it. Each test I expected to fail but was shocked with a C. I finally started studying seriously but it was too little, too late. I remember very little of the written and comprehension portions of the DLPT, but I clearly remember the speaking portion. It was in a building in an area of the base that I rarely entered. I didn't know the person I was speaking to and quickly launched into my story: Who I was, where I was from, what I was studying. I answered his questions and tried not to let my voice shake.

    We had to wait several days to learn our fates. Several days of pacing and trying not to think about what the test would say. No one said a word about the what-ifs. No one said a word about the next schoolhouse or the next base or the next job. When anyone asked how the test had gone for me, I would just stare at them and blink. That bad, huh? I spent those days playing video games with Aaron and struggling to laugh at his jokes. My mind was elsewhere, lost in the unknown.

    The day finally arrived. Only eight of us were left, of the twenty-four we had started with a year and a half prior. One by one we stood in line and took our turn at the small white paper taped to the auditorium wall, inches from the stage where our graduation would take place a week later. One by one a classmate would walk away, in shock. Even the best students had failed. I had failed. The only section that I did remotely well in was speaking. The minimum score to continue in the job was 2/2/1. I had a 1/1/1. I did not know what was next. We were dismissed and told to report in the morning for further instructions.

I left the auditorium and went straight to the smoke pit behind HQ. I sat there for hours, chain smoking an entire pack of cigarettes. I said nothing to anyone, and no one spoke to me. I'm sure my face said it all. I had no idea what tomorrow held. I had no idea what next week held. All I knew was that I was not going to be a linguist. The week prior Soda's class had taken the DLPT, and they had all failed as well. I did not know a single person who had passed. We were all in limbo. We had no idea which way was up. Failure meant not getting the MOS of Marine Linguist, even if you had graduated the course.

The next few days did clear a little of the fog. Since it was a new test, we were going to be given a second chance. We were all going to be grouped back into new classes. Most of my classmates stayed in our old schoolhouse, and some went to join classes that were a few months away from the DLPT. McLeod, a student from Soda's class, and I joined a new refresher course being taught at Fort Ord. Every

day we carpooled out there. Our class was in the basement of the old hospital, near the former mortuary. I got creeped out any time a light flickered. Each morning our class would watch Al Jazeera and

take turns reporting back to our instructors what was going on in the world. Each morning the 2008 American housing crisis was one of the topics, and I worried for my parents back in Tennessee. What would it mean if they, like many other Americans, lost their home?

After six months we were tested, and McLeod and I both still failed. That was it. We would be reclassified. We were sent to casuals until new jobs could be arranged. We both were hoping to stay in the intelligence community. We were smart and could do well in signals or human intelligence. Both worked closely with linguists; it would almost be like we had never left. As it was, the intelligence course at Dam Neck, Virginia would take only those who had twenty-four months left on their contract, and we both had eighteen months remaining. I bargained, saying I would sign a year extension, but since I didn't have an MOS, I was not allowed to sign an extension. I was being forced out of the community I had longed to be a part of, and I was being sent to Administration. The only saving grace was that McLeod was coming with me. We could be miserable together.

If I had it to do all over again, I would have gone straight into the intelligence field. I would still have been sent to DLI due to my scores, but I would at least have had a primary MOS when I failed the DLPT.

When I met Christian, I was on my way out of DLI, being reclassified and in casual status. It had been nearly two years since I had arrived at DLI, so I was viewed as a salty Marine by the NUGs (new useless guys). Christian was one of those.

He was older than the other NUGs and could drink legally, so Aaron and I invited him out with our friends. It was quickly apparent that he was not the kind of Marine you wanted to be around while drunk. I never let him near me when I was alone, and we would get other guys to take him home. This was before we caught him trying to grope one of our friends while she was passed out in our car. We should have reported him then and there, but she asked us not to. After that we stopped inviting him out, but he would show up where we were, seeing as there were only a few bars in town that tolerated Marines.

One of those nights we were out celebrating someone's birthday or promotion. It was the usual group: me, Aaron, Ron, Heath, a few others. We were loud and carrying on, having a great time. It was at Duffy's, of course.

So, we were having a blast and playing darts when Christian walked in. He made his way to our table, but most of us ignored him, so he headed to the bar. After another round or two, I was feeling like a million bucks. I wanted to listen to better music, so I headed over to the jukebox. At this point in the night, the only other woman in the bar was Erin, the bartender. I put the quarters in and chose a few songs. I turned around and was face to face with Christian. I froze. I could smell his foul breath. He said he had always thought I was so pretty, and his hands were on my breasts. He leaned in to try to kiss me, and I reared back a punch. I hit him in the throat and shoved him as hard as I could. I looked over to my friends and saw, with relief, that Aaron had his back to us. The only people who had seen what had happened were Ron, Erin, and a big soldier who often played unofficial bouncer. The soldier and I hefted Christian to his feet and shoved him out of the bar. Erin shouted at him to never come back. Ron kept Aaron occupied. We both knew Aaron would have strangled Christian.

When I went to close our tabs, Erin pointed out that Christian had never closed his. I told her to close it and to give me his card so I could return it. I wanted to speak to him face to face. Come morning, Ron and I headed over to his room and knocked. I did not care that it was nearly noon and that the Marines watching TV in the common room would hear me. Christian opened the door, and I verbally laid into him, yelling up into his face. I told him that if I ever saw him in the bars, I would report his assault and his drinking. The DLI had a rule that if a Marine self-reported alcohol abuse, they would go to rehab and be recycled into another class in their language. But if another Marine reported the alcohol abuse, then the alcoholic would go to rehab and run the risk of being reclassified into another job.

I don't remember all the words I said, but I thought they did the trick. He closed his door, and I started shaking. Ron put an arm around me and led me out of the building. We went to the PX for pizza and Gatorade, then went to wake up Aaron. We agreed that this was something Aaron shouldn't know about. We didn't want him to ruin his career by assaulting another Marine.

I know that my words struck fear into Christian, because when our platoon gathered he couldn't meet my eye, and he steered clear of me when I was hanging out with my friends. About a month later I left the DLI and headed to North Carolina for admin school. I hoped Christian would keep his promise.

He did not. After Vanessa Guillén's murder in April 2020, I started talking about my abuse at the hands of other servicemembers, and I discovered that Christian had continued to be a creep and a pervert. If I had reported him, he wouldn't have gone on to abuse more Marines. I blame myself for their abuse.

Shortly after this incident I had a going-away party and said goodbye to all my friends. I had asked Aaron if he wanted to elope so we would be allowed to stay together after we were done with school and he declined, saying he never wanted to remarry. I responded by breaking up with him, which I greatly regretted the next morning. I had thought he would come back begging, but he did not, and I never saw him again. He was going to go to Hawaii while I was going to North Carolina and then who knew, but for over a year we had had fun together. I believe we could have weathered the distance, but I was too stubborn to admit I was wrong. Deep down I knew I could never change his mind about getting married or having children.

Aaron was a huge part of my twenties. Sometimes I think about the what-ifs. What if he had wanted children? What if we had tried to weather the distance? What if we had gotten married? What if I hadn't been a psychotic bitch? What if I had been able to get orders to Hawaii? What if and what if and what if.

CHAPTER 18

KING OF ANYTHING

"Was that when you came home for the week and we surprised your mom?" I had returned to sitting on the floor, this time playing tug of war with Greyson. Augie had had his fill of wrestling with Grey and was passed out a few feet away, snoring loudly.

"Man, I had forgotten about that! Oh, Mama was so shocked!"

I had decided to take a week of leave to visit Memphis before arriving in North Carolina. Only I didn't tell Mama. I told Dad and Brandy, and they helped me keep it a secret. My flight came in after midnight and Brandy picked me up from the airport. Dad made sure the deadbolt was unlocked before going to bed, and I let myself in. Thankfully Davy didn't bark. I crashed on the couch, and at 6:00 a.m. I was woken up by Mama turning on the kitchen light and saying, "Karen, why did you sleep down here and not in your bed?" When she saw it was me, she screamed and threw her hands in the air. I don't remember much from that visit, but I do remember that!

I had been in the Marines for two years when I was sent to administration school, the worst place for someone like me, at Camp Johnson, North Carolina with McLeod. She and I got to know each other in our refresher course, and at Johnson we were put together as roommates. We both had reputations for drinking too much and causing trouble. This was the first time in my career that I had a reputation for not giving a flying fuck. I was twenty-four and placed with Marines who were still wet behind the ears. McLeod was even more jaded, as she had lost her corporal rank when reclassified. It wasn't her fault that she couldn't pass the DLPT either, but the Marines technically are not supposed to promote students to an NCO position. The DLI was just such a different animal from the fleet. From a DLI Marine's perspective, the fleet was a pink unicorn; it didn't exist.

On our first full weekday we were put in formation, waiting around for the NCOs to show up. As per usual, we were telling stories. The baby Marines were enthralled with McLeod and me and impressed that we were, by their standards, salty. They kept wanting to hear more stories about Monterey, so McLeod told them about my NJP. It seemed to impress them that I had taken a public beating and lived to tell the tale.

I quickly became annoyed by all the questions, and the upside is that none of the students except us and two men, Mason and Crocker, were old enough to drink. Mason was a married Marine who enlisted to help his wife take care of their young son. He was from the Midwest and talked often about his family. He was in my class, and our NCO would frequently chew me out for hanging out with him because of the optics. The more I emphasized that we weren't sleeping together, the angrier she got, stating that denying it would just make people believe the rumor even more. I didn't care what anyone thought because it was the truth, we were just friends. Since no one can NJP you on a rumor, I continued hanging out with him.

Crocker was a supply Marine from Alabama. He often wore his 'Bama baseball cap, and I would try to steal it from him. He had a good sense of humor and easily flirted with any woman. He was short and stocky with mischievous blue eyes. He was the kind of guy that would be down for serious trouble if it involved a pretty woman. He was brilliant, and it baffled me that he was in supply and not intelligence.

Admin school was a miserable few months. I was back in lovely and beautiful North Carolina, but it had a terrible dark cloud over it. We had to get permission to leave the barracks, and leaving the base was usually not allowed due to other people's mistakes. We had the reputation of being alcoholics, but at least we weren't the reason everyone's liberty was cancelled.

We were in a casual status for a few weeks while we waited on our class to start. We marched to the chow hall at 5:00 a.m., then marched to the schoolhouse and sat in an unused classroom. We marched together everywhere. It was restrictive and felt like hell after a year of individuality. In theory the Marine Corps is egalitarian; everyone is treated the same. The saying is that there is no white, brown, or black, only green. We know that isn't true on most bases, but at Camp Johnson it was. We were all to move as one and all needed to do the same thing. We had the same uniform items, same ditty bags (medium-sized camouflage bags), same school supplies. It felt as if I were back in boot camp. If one person forgot an extra uniform item, we all had to go without. Which is how all forty of us ended up marching in forty-degree temperatures, soaked to the bone. One asshat had forgotten to pack his Gor-tex camo poncho. For a few days, he was not a popular Marine.

Admin school Marines were vastly different from DLI Marines. They were always causing trouble and acting foolish. They were boisterous, and many instigated arguments. As a result, the first sergeant forbade talking in the classroom. We had to sit there in silence for eight hours, allowed to speak only when spoken to or at the smoke deck during breaks. Being the nerdy Marine I was, I had brought a small library with me to the camp and asked permission from the sergeant to bring them to the classroom. He granted me permission, and every morning I had my dozen books in my ditty bag. I would sit in the front of the room with a pad of paper, checking out my books to bored Marines. Everyone would return the books at the end of the day. I was pleased that they treated my books with respect. This was before regular folks could afford an iPhone, and it was either play Sudoku, sit in silence, or read. You could get away with a nap if the sergeants were in a good mood.

One morning, Private Nash was last in line and the only book left was A Walk to Remember by Nicholas Sparks. His face fell, but he checked it out because it was better than nothing. Nash was a good ole boy from southern Mississippi, with bright red hair and a smartass grin. He was the last person I would have expected to be interested in a sappy romance, but at the end of the day he came up and asked if he could borrow it for the night. He promised to return it in the morning. I relented, and by morning he had finished it. He had stayed up all night and read it by flashlight.

McLeod, Mason, Crocker, and I all stuck together and counted our blessings that at least there was a bar on the camp. It was a sad little trailer, but at least it had a jukebox and cheap beer. There was no rule that said an of-age Marine couldn't be trashed at the 9:00 p.m. formation, so we were. You were not allowed to have alcohol in your room, and you couldn't go to the smoke pit after nine. Our two other roommates were also reclassified Marines, and one was also from DLI. We were all insomniacs and fledgling alcoholics and stayed up singing bad karaoke and talking to friends on the phone. We had to be in our room, but we didn't have to go to sleep.

After two straight weeks of being on a base lockdown due to stu-

pid Marines, we were annoyed and desperate to get off the base. McLeod and I signed up for a half-marathon at neighboring Cherry Point and had to be escorted by the unit's first sergeant, who was also running. I did not try all that hard in the race. Another time, we were able to leave because Morale, Welfare, and Recreation had planned a trip to Myrtle Beach. We gladly signed up. Unfortunately for me, we had one of our benders the night before and I was nursing a horrible hangover. I slept on the bus, slumped forward, with my head on the bench in front of me and a trash bag in my hands.

My one goal was to get done with admin school with a perfect grade and never again be reclassified or recycled. If you failed too many tests, got sick, or needed to go home, you would have to start completely over. I was nearly done with the school and had only two weeks until graduation. I was on a roll and had 100 percent, when I got a call from my mother that was a punch in the gut: My father had cancer. I pulled my instructors aside and tried hard not to cry as I explained the situation. I could stay and finish out the two weeks and not be there for my dad, or I could take humanitarian leave and go back to Memphis for his surgery. If I chose humanitarian leave, I would have to start over completely. I was torn. The schoolhouse gave me a few days to make up my mind, and there were lots of phone calls with my parents and siblings, late-night texting sessions with Aaron and Luke, and angry tears. I would walk into the woods and scream at trees.

In the end, my parents persuaded me to stay and finish out the school. On the day of my dad's surgery, I paced back and forth at a park and awaited my mom's phone call. The doctors had removed my father's affected kidney, and the margins were clean. There was no more cancer and no need for chemotherapy, just regular check-ups with his oncologist.

Shortly after that we got our orders. The list went down alphabetically, and I waited anxiously for the Cs. I heard bases like "Iwakuni, Camp Lejeune, Camp Pendleton" and was praying for Kaneohe Bay, Hawaii. Then they were in the Cs. "Please get Kbay, please get Kbay," I whispered. I regretted breaking up with Aaron and just knew that if I could be on the same base as him, we would get back together. Every Korean linguist I knew went to Kbay. Then I heard, "Colby." I held my breath, closed my eyes, and wished as hard as I could. "Naval Air Station Joint Reserve Base Fort Worth, Marine Wing Support Squadron 473." I almost swore. Are you fucking kidding me? NAS JRB Fort Worth, formerly known as Carswell Air Force Base, was where I was born on December 13, 1984, in the old base hospital. I was going back where I came from. The only upside was that I would now be only eight hours' drive from Memphis and could visit my family if I wanted. I never did see the fleet. Are we sure it exists?

CHAPTER 19

I NEED NEVER GET OLD

I had left admin school, top of my class, with the best score anyone had ever had. I had missed one answer on one test. Ironically, it was a question on the NJP test. Other than that, my record was perfect. I should have been the Honor Graduate, been promoted, and had my pick of placement. But I was considered fat by the standards, so I received only a "congratulations" and a book about a Marine Corps fight in Vietnam. I was rightfully mad, but I wasn't going to let it follow me to a unit. I was going to the fleet, or so I thought, and I would make a new name for myself. I had joined the Marines to see the world, and I was being sent back home.

As per the regulations, I was checking in wearing my service alphas: the green coat, green pants, and tan shirt that look similar to the Army's green uniform. It was similar enough to cause civilians to confuse the two, and I hated being confused for a soldier. I am a person that is either embarrassingly early or horribly late, so I made sure to get up with enough time to be there before anyone else. I knew better than to show up to my new unit drunk or hung over.

I was sitting with my orders and my service record book, praying no one would notice that my uniform was a little tight. People started coming in, and no one bothered to look my way. I thanked my stars. Until Sergeant Melody walked in, saw me, made a beeline to me, and demanded to know why I was in the wrong uniform. I was confused but stood up, went into parade rest, and asked what she meant. She repeated that I was in the wrong uniform. I asked again for clarification. I was under the impression that all units had Marines wear their alphas, and I was sorry that I hadn't thought to check what this unit required. Her answer made me hate her immediately.

"Women are to always check in in their skirts."

I was furious, because I knew this was wrong. Only a few weeks prior, I had learned that the Marine Corps had stopped requiring women to wear skirts sometime in the 1990s, so I knew that this woman, this NCO, was touting long-expired sexist stereotypes. I calmly told her that I did not have a skirt, as one had never been issued to me. She started to holler and yell, full wannabe drill instructor mode. It was all I could do not to scream back that she was a sexist bitch. I knew I would instantly hate being here if I had to be in her shop. But I had orders to the Marine Wing Support Squadron 473, not Marine Air Group 41, so I was pretty sure I would not have her as my NCO. MWSS 473 fell under the control of MAG 41. The Marine I had come here with stood next to me in shock, silent while I got my ass chewed. I never got to hear her justification of a sexist idea, because Sergeant Sanchez arrived.

"Sergeant Melody, that will be enough. I will take it from here." Sergeant Sanchez was a stocky Marine with a bald head and a Yankee accent. He looked kind, so my hackles came down a little bit. As he ushered me behind a door at the front of the shop, I saw all eyes on me. A shop full of Marines, and no one had bothered to correct the sexist bitch. When I turned to see what office I was in, I was shocked. I was standing in the foyer of the suite of the commanding officer, Colonel Iiams, face to face with several sergeants, a few lower-ranking officers, and several high-ranking enlisted men. In complete shock, I almost forgot I was indoors and nearly saluted the officers. A sergeant at the desk asked if I knew why I was here. I stammered, "Gentlemen, I apologize for being in the wrong uniform. If I can take a moment to go to the store, I will buy a skirt."

They were confused, and I heard a snicker from my left. "Don't worry about her, Marine, she does this to everyone. She likes to put new people on edge. And she's mad because she wanted you for her shop." Now I was even more confused. What was this guy telling me? Did I have the wrong orders? I prayed there was a mistake, that I was really supposed to be in California, Japan, or Hawaii. With the next words, my prayers were dashed. A sergeant at the door introduced himself and said he was from my shop, at the MWSS across the street. Okay, so no mistake, but I could go over there if I was required. Across the street isn't too bad. I had seen the building as I drove in, and it had windows facing the flight line. I could see myself daydreaming and watching the fighter jets and cargo planes take off and land. He further explained that I would be on loan to the MAG for a little while.

At this point Sergeant Baker spoke up. He introduced himself as the Legal Chief and explained that they had been short one legal clerk for a while, and that my unit had agreed to swap me for a few reservists. I would come to hate him, as he was the worst NCO I ever had, but I didn't know this at the time. I was even more confused, because a Legal Clerk was not the same as an Admin Clerk. Legal Clerks were always corporals or above and had to go to a special school to learn all the ins and outs. He further explained that he had been given a heads-up about my test scores from a friend at the admin school and that those, combined with my age and security clearance, made me a perfect candidate for the Legal Shop.

I chose my words carefully. "Thank you, Sergeant Baker. Will I be going to another school? I haven't unpacked yet." I didn't even have a room yet, but it sounded like something I should say. I steeled my nerves for the answer.

"We are working on that. The schoolhouse is only for NCOs, so for now you have the billet but not the rank." I could work with that. The realization was starting to sink in that I was being picked for a special billet just minutes out of school, and I was hoping I didn't come off as cocky. A salty NCO is allowed to be cocky. A little PFC with an NJP on her record is not. My head was buzzing, and I couldn't wait to tell my cousin in law school that I had been picked to work with the Staff Judge Advocate, without any experience other than having been in trouble before.

The gaggle of high-ranking men mentioned my prior trouble and asked me to explain. I told them it had been an error of judgment that I had learned from and would not repeat. The answer seemed to suffice, as they all nodded. One in the back mentioned not trusting a Marine with a perfect record. Had he not been in camis, I would have learned that he was missing a few good cookies. That's something only Marines who have been in trouble say. "Good cookie" is the nickname for the Good Conduct Medal, which Marines earn if they've served thirty-six consecutive months without getting into trouble. I, of course, never got one.

Sergeant Sanchez introduced himself at this point as the Adjutant Clerk and explained that the gunny was his boss as the Chief. He explained that bigger units have more of a separation between the Adjutant's office and the SJA's office, but our unit was tiny, so the two offices worked together. He further explained that I would be dividing my time between working for him and working for Sergeant Baker. I nodded. I had no idea what an adjutant did or what his clerk did. "Working for this office means you will be working directly with the Adjutant, who works directly for the Commanding Officer." He pointed to the two signs above office doors in the foyer. He then pointed out the Executive Officer's office and the office to my left, which belonged to the Sergeant First Class, the highest-ranking NCO in our unit. The realization sunk in that I was being picked to work for the highest ranking and most important men. I felt like an imposter, a fish in a room of sharks, and my mouth went dry.

Sergeant Sanchez further explained that one of my duties for them was to proofread anything that required the Commanding Officer's signature and route it up through the chain to the Sergeant First Class, then the Adjutant, then the XO, and finally the CO. I would meet those two men later in the day. Now the Adjutant, Captain Krauss, poked his head out of his door and asked if he could say a few words. He looked me over and loudly said that he wasn't pleased that I was a woman. Women, apparently, are not to be trusted with this kind of work, and he wouldn't be surprised if I washed out and went back to regular admin. As it was, I worked for him for the rest of my enlistment. All sixteen months of it.

The rest of the day was a blur of people and offices. Sergeant Sanchez took me around to medical and supply. I got assigned a room. Even my room wasn't where I thought it was. The sole Marine barracks was full, so I would be going to the overflow barracks. This worked out just fine, as the overflow barracks was outdoor entry and I could come and go as I pleased and had my own bathroom. I shared it with the room opposite, but it was usually vacant. Men and women don't share bathrooms, and most of the building was geobachelors and Navy personnel. I was shocked to learn that I wouldn't even have room inspections, as these rooms were usually overlooked. I was supposed to stay only until a room opened up, but I stayed nearly a year. After that year I moved into the Doris Miller Barracks, which housed mostly Navy personnel. I never did get moved to the Marine barracks, which was fine. Most lower enlisted folks become squirrelly around a legal clerk, as if it's our fault they're sneaking in alcohol and underage girls and getting DUIs.

By the middle of the day, I was meeting people I should have worked for, and they were not all happy. They grudgingly signed my paperwork for the transfer. I had just two offices to go, and they could have said no. The Executive Officer was a kind man, a pilot who had been grounded due to an unforeseen illness but chose to stay in the Corps to finish out his thirty years with honors. He could have gone on to do anything he wanted, but he loved being a Marine and was not bitter that his diabetes had grounded him. He did not look the part of an adult diabetic. He was in shape and ran marathons. His illness was a fluke, an accident of nature, and it cost him his wings. Of course, I didn't know this on the day I met him. He was an easy man to talk to. This lieutenant colonel asked easy questions of me, eagerly signed my paperwork, and welcomed me aboard. Now just one more hurdle: the CO.

Colonel Iiams was a tall thin man and would have had salt and pepper hair, if he had not been bald. I knocked on his office door, waited to be invited in, walked in, announced myself, and stood at attention. His "at ease" calmed me, and I ventured peeks around when he wasn't looking. He was a highly decorated Marine, a family man, and a Catholic. He was a pilot and had model planes on nearly every surface. His voice was easy to listen to, but I was careful not to relax too much as I answered his questions. For the third time that day I was asked to explain my NJP. He asked why I had been reclassified and why I hadn't been sent immediately to Dam Neck. When I told him, he shook his head. "What a fucking waste! With your scores you should be leading the intel shop. Be sure to request a lateral move when you reenlist." I had to stifle a smile and simply said, "Yes sir, that is the plan." He chuckled, signed my paperwork, and welcomed me aboard.

I would meet the two officers who were to be my lawyers a few weeks later. Both men were reservists but didn't do drill weekend. They were civilian lawyers with practices in town and came in only when we had a case that required their attention. If we didn't have enough of those, they would finish out their required drill time in the summer. Both were powerful and full of knowledge. One, Captain Sheets, became a Texas state representative. We stood on opposite sides of the political aisle, but I was always proud to have worked for him.

On the day I was shown my desk in the cramped legal office, I was mainly happy. I didn't know what kinds of cases I would be working on. I didn't know that I would never go to legal school. I didn't know that I would be loaned out to other legal shops around the area to unfuck their situations. I didn't know that I would never deploy, or that this would be the last assignment of my career. I knew just one thing: that I didn't have to work for Sergeant Melody.

CHAPTER 20

Shivers

I didn't hang out with many of my fellow Marines at the MAG S1 shop. I would like to have been friends with many of them, but my lower rank prohibited it. There were many fine people who worked in the shop. People like Corporal Lopez, who brought his parrot to the company picnic, or Sergeant Hernandez, whose sons I babysat. In a different world we likely would have been friends, but my world was a strange one governed by strict rules. Lower enlisted personnel did not interact with NCOs or Staff NCOs. In a normal Marine shop, there would have been plenty of other lower enlisted Marines to be friends with, but our shop had very few. The only other lower enlisted folks were either reservists, therefore only there once a month, or always in trouble. It made for a lonely time.

Instead, I hung out with sailors, and dated a few of them. The men I loved, and who loved me, are as much a part of my story as the men who abused me. They still hold a place in the back of my heart. At the JRB I gave away more of my heart than I got back, but two men loved me back, each in his own way. Alex was a corpsman on temporary loan from his unit in New York. He was from Colombia and had a sexy accent and a fancy car. We burned bright and fast, and when he left to go back to New York, it was over. We kept in touch for a little while. In 2020 I got a text message from him to let me know he was in Austin for a few days. He was a traveling nurse and passing through on his way to his next place. Covid was still quite new, and I was worried for my husband's health. I declined to meet up but wished him well.

Dosier was another sailor, an aircraft mechanic with the VR-46 Eagles, a fixed wing squadron. We dated only a few times, as I was on the rebound from another sailor whose name I've forgotten. I didn't fall in love with him, but he was good for what I needed. I was horrified when I found out he had been arrested in Japan for the gang rape of a Japanese teenager. He was in town when his ship went into port. I was disgusted. I once trusted him to drive my teenage sister home after we were hanging out. I was too drunk to drive her home, and he offered. I grilled her for days, making sure he hadn't pulled the same shit with her. He had not.

The last sailor I dated was Charlie. I fell hard for him, and we stayed together for years after I left active duty. He held dual citizenship with Costa Rica and had a wonderful accent. Some days he refused to speak English, and I would have to figure out what he was saying using context clues. His father was a World War II Navy veteran who had retired during the Vietnam War. His ship had pulled into Panama and he had gotten off. He could have stayed with the ship until it came home, but he had no interest in returning to the States. Instead, he traveled all over Central America and the Caribbean, trading work for goods. At one point he was a yacht pilot for hire by the wealthy in Jamaica.

By the early 1980s, Charlie Sr. had made his way to Costa Rica. He had not planned on staying there long. Instead, he started sleeping with a young cabana girl and Charlie came along, followed by two more boys. After their youngest was born they decided to get married. Charlie Sr. never spoke a lick of Spanish, and Cecilia never learned English, but they obviously had no trouble communicating. Senior never renounced his U.S. citizenship and made sure to get the boys dual citizenship.

By the time Charlie and I started dating his parents had separated, and Senior was living in the Armed Forces Retirement Center in DC. I never met him face to face, but we did speak on the phone. I loved his Yankee accent and the way he called me "doll." He reminded me of the old crooners my dad listened to. When Senior died at age ninety-two, I cried with Charlie. He was terrified of his mother and took nearly two years to tell her we were dating. I would tease him and remind him that she had no desire to come to the States. It didn't matter.

When I met him he had already been in the Navy for ten years, and his youngest brother was a supply clerk stationed in Norfolk. Charlie was a boatswain's mate by trade but was on what was called shore duty. The Navy doesn't want their sailors to burn out, so after every three-year sea tour they spend a few years on land. His previous ship had been docked in Hawaii, and he had many stories about deployments to South America to assist the Coast Guard taking down drug runners. Since he was a native Spanish speaker, he would help on the "visit, board, search, and seizure" operations and follow closely behind the sailors and coasties with the guns.

The only time I would be invited out with my unit was when everyone was invited out, and that was not often. One such time was a house party to celebrate someone's promotion. It was an on-base party, but I wanted to show off my new car, an older model Z3 that I was quite proud of, so instead of riding with anyone else I drove. I had not planned on staying long and had made plans with Charlie for later in the evening. In my nervousness to fit in, I drank far more than my limit far too early in the evening. My last memory of the night was getting my CDs out of my glovebox for the makeshift deejay. I woke up in my own bed with a massive hangover, wearing another man's shirt and with my own shirt dirty and torn. My first concern was that I had driven drunk, but I couldn't find my keys. I couldn't find my wallet either, so I was unsure how I had gotten into the building, much less my room, without the keycard.

My second concern was whose shirt I was wearing. It was a green-and-white polo shirt that I didn't recognize. I was worried it had happened again. I tried not to think about the tightness in my stomach. I wanted to throw up. I had no memories after retrieving my music the night before. I reached for my phone and called Charlie. I prayed he had driven me home. He had not. My stomach sank further. He told me I had woken him up shortly after 2:00 a.m. by banging on his window. He had let me in the building and into my room, but he said I had been too inebriated to give him any information.

Charlie oversaw Navy housing, and his duty station was in our barracks. He had access to the building's cameras and could help me fill in a few of the gaps, especially how I got home. As I tried not to panic, dwelling on the worst, we reviewed the tapes. They showed a very drunk me stumbling, or should I say falling, out of a car I recognized as belonging to Staff Sergeant Harvey, the S1 Chief. When I saw the footage of him walking me up to the front of the building, the lost moments of the night before came back.

I had drunk far too much and had fallen a few times while trying to dance in the backyard. That must have been where I dropped my wallet. No one noticed just how drunk I was, because everyone else was just as drunk, with the exception of the staff sergeant, who was the designated driver. He suggested it was time for me to go home, but when I got to the barracks I realized my error. We spent the next few minutes trying every door to see if anyone had propped a door open. None were, so I climbed on his shoulders to try to pry open my window. When that failed, he hoisted me on his shoulders again to bang on Charlie's window, and Charlie let me into my room with his master key.

The sheer relief that I hadn't been taken advantage of overshadowed the embarrassment at my inebriation and my pounding hangover. Charlie was able to drive me to pick up my car, though my coworker wasn't pleased when I woke her to retrieve my keys and wallet. I spent the rest of the weekend in bed nursing the cursed hangover.

Many nights Charlie would sneak into my room, or I would sneak into his. The cameras were only on the outside of the building, and we knew his buddies weren't going to rat us out. The rooms were suites with a kitchen, bathroom, and two separate bedrooms. Most of the time I didn't have a roommate to rat me out. We were often broke, so when we couldn't afford the movies we watched TV.

It was Charlie who introduced me to two of my favorite TV shows, *Dr. Who* and *The Big Bang Theory*. When I left active duty, we got an apartment together in town. He was a petty officer and could live off base if he wanted. This gave us access to his BAH (basic allowance for housing), and we were a little better off than previously, but only a little.

CHAPTER 21

VICTORIA'S SECRET

The first year wasn't too bad. Sergeant Sanchez stayed in my corner. He knew what being on weight restrictions was like, and I stayed underweight. I was repromoted to lance corporal and was looking at a meritorious promotion to corporal. I lost it by a few points to a male Marine who later was NJPed for urinating on a building in full view of civilians and children on the one day of the year we're asked to be on our best behavior, the annual Air Show. Processing his case gave me sick joy and also pissed me off. I had to shake my head at the stupidity. That guy had been promoted over me, but he got his just desserts.

Every once in a while we would go on group runs around the base, starting out at the MAG and heading to Lake Worth, before heading back via another street. When we got to the lake, my gunny would point at a large imposing building surrounded by barbed wire and tell the new Marines, "Colby was born there." The Marines would turn and look at me in horror and I would respond, "Gunny, I told you to stop telling people I was born in a prison!" What had been the base hospital was now the Federal Medical Center, Carswell, a federal women's medical prison.

Sergeant Sanchez took me on bike rides along the Trinity Trails, helped me make plans for my diet that wouldn't kill me, and gave me tips for shaving inches off my waist. His tips helped, and I was making weight. He joked that I needed to hang a "Procrastination on Your Part Does Not Constitute an Emergency on Mine" sign on the wall behind me. He would stifle laughter when I stood my ground. High-ranking NCOs and junior officers would come in and demand that the CO sign immediately whatever was in their hand. I would ask them what it was, and usually it was something they had known about for a week and only just typed up. I would remind them that three other people needed to sign it before the CO, and that he would sign it when he got to it. This was assuming there were no spelling errors or spacing problems. The Marines are sticklers about spaces and proper typing. If it was someone I secretly liked, I would retype it and route it for signature. If it was someone I didn't like, or a repeat offender, I would red pen it and tell them to redo it. Watching me take on these people who vastly outranked me was like a little show that my NCOs and some of the officers liked to watch. It takes nerves of steel and giant balls to stand up to these giants.

If it was legal paperwork, it required extra signatures. Those were my favorite "no's", and they usually involved an NJP that was happening that afternoon, usually for something stupid. I got pleasure telling the staff sergeant or gunny that the NJP would not be happening until the office had the chance to review the case. That is not to say there were not cases that required my immediate attention. For those, I would drop whatever else I was doing and start the research for the Staff Judge Advocates. NJPs didn't require the attention of the lawyers, but some offenses were so severe that they required a court martial. There are men in Leavenworth today based on the research I did for their cases. But the little ones, usually skipping a drill weekend or showing up drunk while underage, I had no problem shooting down if they showed up the same morning they were scheduled to be held. Those cases would have to be handled the next day or the next drill weekend.

When Sergeant Sanchez transferred to Japan, Sergeant Baker took over as Adjutant Clerk and Corporal Torrez moved in to be Legal Chief. That was a job that should have been mine, but the gunny wanted an actual NCO in the billet. Corporal Torrez was an incompetent fool, a meathead who cared little for anyone who couldn't bench press three hundred pounds. He often missed paperwork that required his review, then would hold up the process because the date was wrong. I was tired of those asschewings, and he would happily throw me under the bus. I hated him to my bones and hate that he got to go to Hawaii after the JRB, and I still spit when I say his name. Having him on my back made my situation with Sergeant Baker even worse. He would lie and the others would believe him. They believed I was lazy, despite my processing nearly two hundred dishonorable discharges for the neighboring 14th Marines. After being the only shop that received 100 percent on a difficult office inspection by the 4th Marine Division, I was loaned out to other units to unfuck their legal messes. 14th Marines had two hundred Marines who had not been showing up for drill weekend, some for years. But sure, Corporal Torrez, I was a lazy Marine.

It might sound mean to say that Sergeant Randy Baker should never have been in charge of anyone, but it's the honest truth. On some things he did well, but most he failed miserably. He was a good Marine, smart and knowledgeable. We both knew the Uniform Code of Military Justice backwards and forwards. We could quote it like others quote the Bible. It helped us in our jobs, making sure the offending Marine got what was coming to him. And sometimes we used it to save a Marine who had been dealt a bad hand.

Sergeant Baker never had my back the way an NCO should. He would talk about me within earshot and had spies among the ranks. I needed him to have my back, and he failed. One drill weekend I came up to the unit earlier than anyone else, like usual, and saw a situation that required immediate unfucking. Two new Marines sat waiting for the S1 shop to open. One looked perfectly okay in his alphas, but the other was what caused me to pause. He was wearing a green alpha coat, woodland cami bottoms, and dress shoes. He also still had his cover on, indoors. Hardass Colby came out in full force, and I had both of them at parade rest. After chewing out the offender, I turned on his friend.

"Why the hell did you not stop this idiot?"

"Ma'am, we didn't want to be late."

"I'm not a ma'am, I'm a lance corporal."

"Aye ma'am, uh, I mean, aye lance corporal."

I turned back on the offending Marine and asked where the hell his proper clothes were.

"I lost it."

"You lost it. You lost your pants?!"

I snatched up his orders and was flabbergasted.

"How the hell did you lose your pants?! You literally just graduated Fireman School yesterday! Did you graduate like this?"

I dismissed them and told them to either borrow pants from someone or go buy them. I told them if I saw them again in this state, I would chew them out again. Chewing them out was really the only thing I could do. Three hours later, an irate sergeant came stomping into the shop, demanding to know why I had made them go to the uniform shop and made them late checking in. I attempted to respond, but he continued to yell at me. Words like "lazy" and "fatass" came out and I stood there, stunned. He was friends with Baker. When he stomped off, Sergeant Baker asked what that was all about. He advised me that I was in the wrong and deserved the asschewing. The whole time I thought to myself, "What the actual fuck is going on?" The Marine Corps I grew up in required lance corporals to correct misbehaving manchildren where we could. How was it suddenly my fault that the kid had lost his pants after less than twenty-four hours?

Another time, I was at the point where I could no longer be kicked out for being overweight. I had a few months left, but to be kicked out you're required to have three six-month periods of being on weight restriction. I had two, and I had decided that I was not reenlisting. I was standing on the cold scale, and I didn't care what it said. Another female Marine was also there weighing in. She was crying about not making weight, and I reminded her: "Just think, in a few months both of us can be as fat and happy as we want." She laughed. But our monitor, Sergeant Melody, ratted me out to my boss. I got an asschewing for being so cavalier about my weight and was given two extra miles to run that day. Mind you, I was less than 160 pounds. Yes, at five foot two that's considered overweight, but the tape standards did not take into consideration my large boobs or that my neck was smaller than it should have been. If I could have traded big boobs for a bigger neck, I would have. Just an extra inch in my neck, and I would not have had a problem with the taping and weigh-ins.

Standing half naked in front of several NCOs was one of the most humiliating parts of my career. It happened not once, but weekly for the better part of a year. I checked in to Naval Air Station Joint Reserve Base in April 2009 and left in August 2010. When I checked in, I was slightly overweight at 150 pounds and was rather angry that I had the position of honor graduate, and the meritorious promotion, stolen from me because of my weight. I was bitter and angry for being reclassified to administration after two years at the DLI, and I was primed for a fight with anyone. As it was, the only people on the JRB to fight with were people who held my career in their hands, jaded and disillusioned NCOs and officers who were overjoyed that there was a little E2 joining the unit that they could bully.

No matter how hard I tried, I was unable to lose the extra ten pounds. Instead, I gained weight every week. I would get up early for the gym and work out prior to group PT. One time a captain from one of the squadrons told my captain he should be proud of my dedication and drive. Captain Krauss responded by saying, "Oh yeah? If she's in the gym so often, why is she so fucking fat?" I felt fat and disgusting, standing in my underwear on a cold scale every week. Returning to my office I felt dejected, and I waited on the yelling to begin from Captain Krauss. I could barely meet my sergeant's eye when he asked how the weigh-in had gone, and I dreaded the extra PT that would follow. I was hungry from starving myself all week and knew I would crack come 5:00 p.m. on Friday, when Charlie would pick me up, take me out for a beer at an off-base bar, and persuade me to eat something. I knew I would cave and binge all weekend, only to try to throw it up. If throwing up didn't work, there was always a box of laxatives. Or I could just guzzle Epsom salts and warm water. I can still taste the horrid combination when I think about those days, and I want to throw up.

Sunday night I would dread having to wake up for PT. My boss was a six-foot-tall marathon-running hardass, and I wouldn't be able to keep up, and I hated making him turn around. Eventually he gave up on me and left me to my own workout schedule. I had no guidance on how to properly work out. I would volunteer for phone duty during lunch, to prevent myself from eating in the chow hall. I was proud of the work I was doing for the base legal office, even if it made me unpopular among my peers. But no one saw the dedicated and brilliant paralegal. All they saw was an overweight slob who was obviously too lazy to lose it.

I was slowly killing myself for a Marine Corps that didn't care if I was alive or dead. I felt all alone on a small base of mainly reservists and felt comfort in my apathy. I didn't care that I wouldn't be able to reenlist. I didn't care that I never got to see the fleet. I didn't care that my hope of being one of the few female master gunnery sergeants was over. I just didn't care. All I needed was to survive until the end of my enlistment. I would count the number of days I had left and pray that I wouldn't be kicked out. I had given up my entire life for the promise of free college, and I was on the verge of losing all of it. I dreaded the civilian world if I washed out of the Corps.

Looking back now, I cringe at these angry memories. I know that if I had had just one person in my chain of command on my side, I would have made a fantastic Marine with a long and decorated career. If I had had a nutritionist or a therapist, I would have learned that when under immense stress our bodies produce cortisol, making it nearly impossible to shed the pounds. The emotional and psychological abuse that I suffered under the ever-watchful eye of a horrible captain cost me my career, and I'm not ashamed to point the finger at him.

I've been embarrassed and ashamed that the weight continued to pile on after my exit from the Marines. I would go months before telling someone I was a veteran, and I saw the looks from other veterans when I dared attend an event. I've heard the fat jokes and internalized them. I've attempted to erase portions of my twenties and have invalidated my own experiences. My hope is that, in voicing my own truths, I will never be the butt of a fat joke again. But I know that is not possible while Marines like John Krauss are able to serve out their careers.

Twelve years have passed since I was last forced to stand on a scale with my career on the line, but I can still feel the cold metal beneath my feet. I can still feel myself sucking in my fat rolls. I can still feel the anxiety rising in my stomach. I can still hear the frustration in my monitor's voice and the grumbling down the hall that she has to see me again next Friday. I can still feel the disgusted eyes of my unit looking down on me as I walk down the hall. I can still taste the bile when I tried throwing up each night. I still hold on to the shame. And the anger.

CHAPTER 22

WORLD SPINS MADLY ON

My time at the MAG was not entirely spent trying to lose weight. Working in the legal office afforded me the opportunity to work on complex cases with two lawyers or, as we called them, staff judge advocates. We had many cases of spousal or child battery, and even one incident that involved a reservist attempting to smuggle weapons in from Mexico. We had a Marine who tried to bring an arsenal onto base to kill his gunny. He was almost not searched at the gate, and we can only imagine what would have happened had he made it past the checkpoint. One of the hardest cases I worked on was when a friend was accused of assaulting his wife. It was hard to put my personal biases aside, but I managed. That case paled in comparison to a child molestation case where the father is now serving life in prison in Leavenworth.

My day-to-day duties were split between offices, but I managed to keep them all straight. I liked working in the fast-paced environment. I should have thrived. Had I been in a civilian office I would have been the star, but my weight held me back from any significant career advancement in the Marines. Another factor was my lack of deployments. Any time one of the subordinate units was deploying, I would volunteer. And each time, I would be turned down. I was told I was too valuable and needed at the MAG. In other words, no one wanted to train a replacement. I would argue that this was 2009 and I could support the MAG electronically. I argued that Marines make mistakes in the field, and I could do all their legal paperwork from there. I argued and argued but was turned down each time.

By the time I decided not to reenlist, I had given up hope for a deployment. I was dejected that I was going to be one of the few Marines who had enlisted during a time of war but stayed stateside. It became a running inside joke between Charlie and me. And then, one uneventful afternoon in May 2010, I was called into Captain Krauss's office. He sat behind his desk as I stood in front of it, waiting to be told why he had called me in.

"You are being given the opportunity to go to the field."

I perked up. The field! Finally! Where was I going? Iraq? Afghanistan? Morocco? I quickly ran through the list of places I knew we had units deploying to and waited patiently for the captain to give me my orders.

"You are going to Hawthorne, Nevada."

I was confused. I had never heard of Hawthorne and wasn't sure what the field work entailed.

"You will be assisting in the training of reservists who are part of an upcoming Afghanistan deployment."

Huh. I was stumped. Why was I being called to train reservists when I had never deployed, much less been to Afghanistan?

"I see, sir. Thank you. May I ask why I have been picked to train them?"

"You can teach them Arabic."

I was confused. Arabic is spoken in twenty-two countries across North Africa and the Middle East, from Morocco to Iraq, but not in Afghanistan. The languages share a similar alphabet and the Quran, but that's where the similarities end. It would be like a French teacher being called upon to teach German, simply because they share the same letters and the Bible.

"Thank you, sir, but Arabic is not one of the languages spoken in Afghanistan."

"Are you arguing with me? Of course it is."

Here is where I stopped. I knew I was correct, but I did not feel like arguing any further and risking an insubordination claim by my boss. I figured I would let it slip to Lieutenant Johnson in the intelligence shop that it might be good for the next intelligence brief to include a basic crash course in the languages of Afghanistan.

I had a week to prepare for Hawthorne. I needed to double check that I had all of my appropriate gear and had to check out sleeping bags and the like from supply. I needed to move my dog, Mr. Gibbs, from my grandmother's house to my sister's house and update Corporal Torrez on the status of my cases. I was only going to be gone for three weeks, but there was a lot to do. I still had no idea what I would be doing when I got there, but I figured someone would fill me in.

Hawthorne, Nevada is a tiny town in the desert and home to an almost empty ammo depot. Its primary purpose these days is training, due to its proximity to Bridgeport, California and the Marines' Mountain Training Center. Over the course of six weeks in June and July, reservists from around the country would be completing their annual training and getting ready for the coming deployment. The training would be divided into three sections, rotating out units so that no reservist was there for more than two weeks. It was to be divided into advance party, main party, and rear party. I was there for the advance party and half of the main party. These sessions were supposed to be mockups for a full deployment, including pilots, infantrymen, and all the support staffs. The pilots and support staff were in Hawthorne, while the infantry was in Bridgeport.

There were only thirty other Marines on the C-130 with me when we left the JRB. We stopped off in New Orleans and at Twentynine Palms, California to pick up supplies needed for the training, and we touched down in Hawthorne a few hours before nightfall. There was nothing there except a few abandoned buildings, dust, and three hundred other Marines from around the country. We were there to set up camp for the main party and had two weeks before our three hundred would grow to a thousand. There was going to be a lot to build. But the first few nights were going to be spent on cots in the largest of the abandoned buildings.

We dropped our gear and grabbed cots. Marines would be arriving through the night, and they needed places to sleep. The ground was not an option because of snakes, scorpions, and other desert critters. I claimed a cot smack in the middle of my thirty comrades and felt happy to be away from Captain Krauss for three weeks. There was nothing else to do until lights out, so a few of us continued the game of spades we had started on the plane. There was a tap on my shoulder.

"Hey, Marine, we set up an area for us over there." The woman, a sergeant, pointed to a wall of MRE boxes. "You should join us."

"Thanks, but I would rather sleep here."

"Don't you want privacy to change?"

"No, I can do that in my sleeping bag."

"Don't you want to sleep away from all these men?"

I looked her square in the eye and paused.

"No offense, Sergeant, but I don't know you. I know them. Boxes of MREs aren't going to stop anyone if they want to come for me. These guys will."

Safe to say I did not win her over as a friend, but I had a point. I knew all too well that isolating myself could lead to more trouble than staying with the pack.

Over the next few days, ten-person tents had to be set up by the hundreds, with cots directly on the sand. There were special tents that were double lined to keep the sand out of the computers. There were giant tents to park Humvees under. The chow hall tent was so big it took thirty Marines to raise. Several raised wooden structures were built that eventually became the showers, but for the first week we were left to baby wipes and canteen baths.

There were only four women that first week, and to bathe was a team effort. We could do it only at night, away from prying eyes. Three women would stand guard while the fourth got clean. We would strip down and wash ourselves with splashes from the water bull, a 400-gallon mobile water container. Then we would switch. Bathing took nearly an hour, but we happily gave up an hour of sleep to be mostly clean.

I ran out of cigarettes early on but was able to bum enough to keep me going until a roach coach arrived. If there was a job that needed to be done, I volunteered. The days were scorchers, and the nights were freezing.

Once everything had been built, I turned my attention to admin work that needed to be done. My first thirty guys were going home, and I wanted to get a jump on their travel paperwork and orders. My counterpart back in Fort Worth was quite pleased to not have to do this, and the guys were pleased that they were not going to have to sit around in S1 waiting for it to be done. They all had civilian lives and jobs to get back to and did not want the delay. By the time the main body arrived, there were permanent sweat stains on my camis and I smelled as bad as everyone else. On the first night one of the new batch, a Marine with a New Jersey accent, called me out in formation.

"What, is pushing pencils so hard that you break a sweat?"

Before I could defend myself, a sergeant I had never spoken to piped up.

"This Marine worked harder than anyone else these last few weeks," he informed the New Jersey newcomer. "She attached herself to the combat engineers and helped build most of the base. You should be thanking her."

I could barely hold back my grin. It was nice to be noticed and praised for work, even though the truth is that I just never know what to do with myself when I'm bored.

When I returned from the field and had cell service again, I saw I had a voicemail from my mother asking me to call her as soon as I could. From the tone I could tell it was bad news, and I put it off to the next day. It was Sunday and Charlie and I hadn't seen each other in weeks and wanted alone time.

The next day I had taken phone duty for lunch again and was sitting at the desk in the CO suite. I waited for everyone to leave to call Mama. She informed me that my nine-month-old puppy, Mr. Gibbs, had died at my sister's house. I was stunned and numb.

Mr. Gibbs had gotten very sick and was in extreme pain. The vet thought it might have been parvo but wasn't sure, as none of my sister's other dogs were sick. Karen said he didn't make it through the night, and the vet wouldn't give her his collar and tags, as he wasn't sure what had made him sick. Mr. Gibbs had thrown up multiple times, and the sick had gotten on his collar. The vet wasn't sure if it was contagious, so he wouldn't turn them over.

Karen and her boyfriend (later husband) Steven had buried him in the backyard next to our family dog, Davy, who had died a few months earlier. Karen was worried that I would be angry with her, so she had Mama call. I was not mad at her.

I hung up and started crying uncontrollably. Every time I thought I could stop, more tears would fall. I had finally gotten to the point where I could stop, when Colonel Iiams walked in. He saw my swollen face and looked around to see if anyone else was in the office. Finding no one, he approached my desk and asked what was wrong. I burst into tears again and choked out that my dog had died when I was in the field. His face softened and he came around to pat my back. He said he understood the pain and explained that his dog had died a few months earlier, and that it had been really hard on his girls. In that moment he was not my commanding officer, but an empathetic father figure.

After a few minutes of patting my back and letting me cry, he handed me a tissue and told me to go wash my face and have a cigarette. He assured me he would watch the phones. After a ten-minute break, I had regained my composure and went back to the office. I walked in to see Colonel Iiams on the phone, with his feet propped up on my desk. Sergeant Baker was standing to the side in disbelief, and his face became angry when he saw me walk in. When Colonel Iiams hung up the phone he cut Sergeant Baker off before I could get an asschewing.

"Lance Corporal Colby got some bad news and is having a really rough day. She is going to work at your desk in the Legal Office, and you will man the phones here."

I lowered my eyes and thanked him and scurried off before any more questions were asked. It took me seven years before I could get another dog, Greyson.

Knowing the UCMJ so well is what made it possible for me to leave the Marines after one enlistment, instead of staying in for twenty years. The plan had to be thrown out because I knew no one would fight for me the way I fought for complete strangers. I fought tooth and nail to make sure that an NCO from a subordinate unit wasn't thrown on his ass for not making weight. I saw myself in him. He was a stellar Marine, held a first class PFT, and had a career he was proud of. The new weight standards, namely taking away the extra four percent body fat from First Classers, had hurt many Marines. I fought for him to get the honorable discharge he deserved. And when the fight was over, I told my career counselor to cancel my request to rejoin the intel community. I was most certainly not going to reenlist.

Part Three

The Times They Are A-Changin'

CHAPTER 23

Last Love Song

My decision to leave the Marines was an easy one, but my parents were disappointed I wasn't returning to Memphis. They were so proud of their Marine daughter, but Mama said she had been holding her breath for four years. She could finally breathe. I could use my GI Bill at the University of Memphis, like my dad. Or I could go to Christian Brothers University or Rhodes College, both incredible schools. But I did not want to go back to the life I had left behind in Memphis. Charlie was in Fort Worth, and so was Texas Christian University. It was important for me to use my GI Bill at a private school, or one that had a reputation for rigorous academics. The new Post-9/11 GI Bill had just been instituted, and it meant private schools were now open for more people without having to incur any costs. I wanted TCU.

I was happy to be starting college days after I started terminal leave. I started off at Tarrant County Community College because I was worried it would be a repeat of my time at Middle Tennessee State. It was not. I excelled and stayed until nearly all of my core credits were completed, although there were several starts and stops. There was confusion with my advisor and the GI Bill certifying office, and some of the classes were not supposed to be covered. The certifier would amend my certification, and I would owe both the VA and TCC. I would have to sit out a semester while Charlie and I tried to pay them back. At one point I owed the VA over five grand. I had wanted to get my associate's degree but was told I had to take remedial math. It had been too long since I took, and passed, AP Calculus, so I left one credit short. I was happily fat, and glad that in civilian life it is not socially acceptable to terrorize someone over their appearance.

Charlie and I had been dating for six months when I got out, but he still had two and a half years on his orders. Our first apartment was fifteen minutes to base. We were still broke and only ever had one working car. When we would get mine fixed, his would break down, and vice versa. I would get up with him at 5:00 a.m. and sleep in the car while he drove to meet his squad for PT. It was fortunate that I knew the route by heart, because one time I forgot my glasses and drove back with everything blurry. I would go to class and use the wi-fi in the library, then go back and pick him up in the evening. It was tiring, but it was what we had to do.

In the mornings Charlie would always shower before leaving the apartment, which confused me. Once I asked why he showered before PT, and I loved his response: "It's so I don't pass away at the wheel." I chuckled and corrected him. "Charlie, it is pass out. Pass away is to die." Despite speaking English fluently, he often made mistakes with colloquial phrases. He was more comfortable with Spanish, and I loved when he spoke to me in his native tongue. I imagined having little bilingual babies with him.

Our relationship had its ups and downs. Our three years were spent scraping by. Being a poor college student was not unlike being a poor Marine, except as a college student no one is going to put a roof over your head and feed you three square meals a day. There were times when we didn't have electricity or water, but at least we always had the roof. I would always leave our porch light on so I could see if we still had electricity when I pulled into our parking lot. Also, I didn't want to be surprised when I opened the door. I never liked it when I opened the door to darkness. I kept a flashlight in my car.

Living in poverty stressed us, but we made do. Charlie had grown up in worse poverty and was used to it. At one point his family's home had dirt floors. He and his brothers often had holes in their shoes. After sixth grade he left school to help make money. He held various jobs, including working on a coffee plantation and being a caddy at a local golf course. His English helped him score that gig, as most of the golfers were wealthy Americans. He always told me the richer the customer, the worse the tipper. Charlie got his GED after moving to the States at nineteen and joined the Navy shortly after.

We would lie in bed and plan out our life for after I finished school. We would get married, start a family, and reap the benefits of patience. I wanted to go to law school. We would be a lawyer and a career Navy man. We wanted three children, two boys and a girl. We hoped one of the pregnancies would be twins. We would have the first between graduating and starting law school, and the other two after I passed the bar.

Through these years I stayed in touch with a few of my DLI friends, but one by one they left me behind to go do wonderful things in the arts or the corporate world, and I felt like I was just spinning in a circle. But I had Charlie, and I would text often with Aaron and Luke. Aaron had gotten remarried after all and was somewhere in the middle of a cornfield trying to make a name for himself in comedy. Luke had a few more years in the Marines and was looking forward to a deployment. We had last seen each other in Monterey at my going-away party in 2009, but we texted almost every day. He called us sinking ships due to our romantic missteps, and I loved him. If I had ended up in North Carolina, I would have wanted to date him. I would have married that man, if only he had asked. Charlie was aware of my feelings for Luke and never held it against me, knowing I was not going to act on them.

On February 12, 2011, we were back to only one car. Mine had a blown radiator, and we were saving to get it fixed. It was a Saturday, and Charlie had to work the drill weekend. I drove him, then headed to my parents' house to do laundry. My parents had moved back to Texas the previous July, and my youngest sister was a freshman at Grand Prairie High School, the very school I should have attended had we not moved to Memphis. When I had left active duty and decided to stay in Fort Worth, they took it as a sign to come home, as they would say. I liked having them close by, and not just for the free laundry and wifi.

This particular Saturday was like any other. Laundry, hanging out with the family, watching TV. I wanted to send a note to my friends who had been in Afghanistan for a few weeks with the 2nd Radio Battalion. I had much to tell them about the freak snowstorm the week before and how I thought of them when I saw a Marine unit on TV during the Super Bowl. I asked my mother if I could use her computer and logged on to Facebook. As I scrolled through my feed, I saw an alarming number of my former fellow DLI students posting "Rest in Peace." One of them was from Aaron, and it had a link to an obituary. My world screeched to a halt when I saw Luke's face. I screamed. My parents came running in to see why I was screaming. Mama said she hated the first thing that popped into her head: "Thank God it was not my child." She then cried for Luke's mother.

Luke had been killed by an IED the week before, a month shy of twenty-five. I read the words in his obituary, and they didn't make any sense. How could he be gone? How could life continue forward, when one of the kindest and most talented of men had died? In one moment I was happy, looking forward to sending Luke and my other friends a silly message about snow and football, and in the next I was grieving a dear friend. My brain couldn't comprehend the two, and I was in a fog. I cried more tears than I knew I could produce and, when I thought I was done, I cried some more. I don't remember the drive back to base to pick up Charlie. I do remember screaming that night as Charlie rocked me on our couch. My sister Karen's wedding was a few months away. As I helped plan the last-minute details, I would remember that somewhere else another sister was helping plan her brother's funeral, and my heart would fall.

I was angry at the Marine Corps. Luke was a Russian linguist, so why the fuck was he on a patrol in Afghanistan? Needs of the Marine Corps. Why would the Marines spend so much money on a linguist, only to throw his life away? Every Marine a rifleman. I stayed angry for many years. I was angry for finding out on Facebook, angry that he was gone, angry at him for dying. I was angry at myself for being so poor that I couldn't afford to go to his funeral. I missed my friend. I missed his text messages, telling me he was in love again. I missed his voice, even at 5:00 a.m. on my birthday. I missed his sense of humor and our deep talks about things that matter. I missed him.

What I wouldn't give to hear Luke's voice today. He is buried in Arlington National Cemetery, an honor rarely reserved for a regular Marine, but he was the first Marine linguist killed in a war since Vietnam, and they wanted to honor his death. DLI has a building named after him now. His death left a wake too large to describe, and I still see him in the faces of men when I'm walking through a crowd. I will always remember him as a young man, strumming his guitar, taking shots of Wild Turkey. When I visit him in Arlington, I leave half of a small bottle of Wild Turkey, taking the other half myself. It's the only time I drink that stuff.

Charlie helped put me back together after Luke's death, and our relationship became stronger for it. We were always putting each other back together. We took turns falling apart.

In November 2011, shortly after his father's death, we were hit with another devastating blow. After two and a half years, my father's cancer had returned and metastasized all over his body. We were told this would kill him and there was nothing to be done. It was still renal cell carcinoma, which meant that traditional chemotherapy is utterly useless against it. Chemo works only on fast-growing cancer cells, and his was a slow-growing type. Over the next many years, he fought cancer and got sicker and sicker. He was involved in different studies, and the MD Anderson Cancer Center in Houston gave him a fighting chance. He told people that he wasn't dying of cancer, he was living with it. Through it all he continued to teach, and I worked hard so he could see me graduate.

I would often drive him to his appointments in Houston and would study in the hospital. I had empathetic professors who allowed me to turn in my assignments over email. A friend would give me the class notes, and I would catch up during office hours. I was grateful to them for their compassion.

Charlie and I weathered so many storms. We survived poverty with one working car. We survived me going to college. We survived his father's death and my father's terminal diagnosis. We survived the loss of our first and only pregnancy. The pregnancy came three years earlier than planned, but we were thrilled to become parents. We were going to name him Lucas. Or we were going to name her Charlotte and call her Charlie, like her daddy and late grandfather. Just as we were getting used to the idea of being parents, we lost the baby. Hearing the doctor say he couldn't find the heartbeat nearly killed me.

Charlie stayed by me through this period of poverty and never judged when I couldn't pay a bill. At least once a semester the lights would be turned off, and I would scrape together enough money to turn them back on. As long as I still had a roof over my head, I could deal with no electricity. The worst was when it would be turned off in the winter. The VA never really pays anyone enough to survive, and you weren't paid during breaks, hence the lights off and late rent in January.

After so many horrible events one after the other, Charlie's mental health suffered. He was not a religious person, so I urged him to speak with a mental health professional rather than a chaplain. I assured him it would be okay, since there was doctor-patient confidentiality. Boy was I wrong. After a thirty-minute session with a Navy shrink, the doctor said he was bipolar and started his medical discharge paperwork. We were floored. Knowing what I know now about mental health, I know it is impossible to have a diagnosis after thirty minutes. It took me months and months of appointments with the VA for me to get my own mental health diagnosis.

Charlie had orders to Rota, Spain, a placement we were thrilled with, and we made plans to elope so I could join him. But the medical discharge put a halt to those. Having worked in legal, I knew the ins and outs of medical discharges and helped him fight it. We sought help from a civilian psychologist and together built a case for him to stay. In the end, his case went all the way to a board in DC and was thrown out. He was staying in the Navy, but his orders to Spain had been given to someone else. He was back in the "needs of the Navy" situation. His monitor suggested a perfect placement: the USS *Constitution* in Boston was in need of a boatswain's mate. This was a rare opening, and you had to volunteer for it. It was a strict position and few sailors qualified. Charlie was one who qualified.

The USS *Constitution* is an American Revolution frigate and was one of the six original Naval ships. It served as a museum in Boston Harbor but would leave port for special two-week floats. The sailors wore period uniforms and acted as tour guides, but also helped with the upkeep of the 215-year-old wooden-hulled frigate. Today she is the world's oldest naval vessel still afloat. The Navy still owns the ship, and she has a standing crew of eighty sailors.

I begged Charlie to take it. It was perfect, as I was finishing up at TCC and needed to pick a university. Boston had so many, and I knew I could go to one. We would have been there long enough to get a bachelor's degree and could take a year off before going to law school. But Charlie didn't want to go to the East Coast. He told me that once you got on the East Coast, you were usually stuck and would end up at Norfolk. He never wanted to be stationed there. So instead, he declined his monitor's offer and asked for different orders.

He was given orders to San Diego, which we could live with. But a sailor who had orders to Hawaii had a sick child and needed to be nearer a children's cancer hospital. His monitor asked Charlie's monitor if he would switch with the other sailor, and both men agreed. Charlie was going back to Hawaii, and I had a choice to make. At this point I had been accepted to TCU. I also had other prestigious schools pursuing me, like Cornell and NYU. I could go with Charlie, or I could stay. In the end, I chose TCU over Charlie. I chose Fort Worth over Hawaii. It was the end of me and Charlie. We survived so much in our three years, but we never survived the distance. We broke up a few months after he left, just before my spring break.

CHAPTER 24

Nothing More

I got a job at TCU in the Veterans Services office, working for a fantastic former Marine named Ricardo Avitia. I was getting the hang of things and helping him double check that the courses veterans were taking matched their degree plans. We had about a hundred veterans and two hundred dependents to get through. I was familiarizing myself with the students we had and making sure their files had everything we needed. Everything was going smoothly – until my hands touched a file in front of me with the name "Baker, Randy."

My throat went dry, and I coughed. Ricardo looked up and asked if I was okay. I told him that I recognized a name from my Marine days, and it had startled me. I quickly saw that we were in different degree plans, and prayed I would never see him on campus. A few days later he walked into the office, and I was right back to three years prior, back in the cramped office in the MAG, and I couldn't breathe. Thankfully he only lasted a semester before going back to Chicago, and I happily haven't seen him since.

At TCU I found lasting friendships with other veterans. I met Elyana and Quinn on my very first visit, before I was even accepted. Elyana was a Navy veteran and had many stories of life on a ship. She was protective of her food due to her time afloat and would stab a bitch with a fork if they ever tried to take food off her plate. Quinn was an Army combat veteran who had also been in legal. We've often swapped stories about the stupid shit our platoonmates would do.

In my last semester I met Arthur and Steve. Arthur was a Navy submariner and I thought he was incredibly hot. At the time I was not seriously dating anyone, having entered my second "hoe phase," and had rules about sleeping with fellow veterans at TCU. But that didn't stop me from admiring good-looking men. Anyway, he was engaged. We lost touch after graduation but reconnected when he moved to Austin a few years after me. Steve was an infantry Marine I met at a Marine Corps cake-cutting ceremony the school put on. We hit it off immediately and often hung out at each other's apartment. We would crash on each other's couch and laugh at our shared bad taste in partners. Steve is still a major part of my life, and Karen's kids call him Uncle. I'm not sure if they're aware he isn't actually our brother. He and his partner travel with us on family vacations and, despite the distance, we visit each other often. He was the best man at my wedding. He is off doing super cool things with his PhD in mechanical engineering.

Being a student at TCU in my late twenties was an interesting mix of confusion, pride, and exhaustion. Unlike most of my classmates, I came from a background of poverty and had spent time in an inner-city high school. I had never been to a private school, and I often felt I was floundering. I was also dealing with real-world situations, years beyond my classmates, not to mention all of my trauma. I had been in the Marines, had already lost my first pregnancy, and had a terminally ill parent. I used to go to Wednesday Mass with the Catholic student group. Their troubles seemed small compared to mine, and I didn't fit in. Many days I felt like I was underwater and struggling to breathe. I didn't let on about this to anyone. I would see a friendly classmate, and their smile would be enough to keep me above water for the day. At one point I felt it was too much and reached out to the president of the Catholic student group to talk about what I was going through. He blew me off, so I stopped going to Mass. Instead, I took up my place at the local bar and was there before and after class, sometimes during. Even when I was making As and Bs in my classes, I still felt as if I were failing.

Early on at TCU I fell into another alcoholic phase. Elyana, Quinn, and I would drink our younger classmates under the table and cause all sorts of ruckus. Our favorite bar was Buffalo Brothers on University Drive, next to the bookstore. We became friendly with the staff due to our generous tipping and would often get stronger drinks than the other patrons. We were often invited to go to house parties with the staff and to join them at their tables when they were off duty.

Many times, I would be at Buffalo Brothers when it opened and start my day with a few drinks before going to class. I was doing relatively well in my classes, and my professors never seemed to notice that I was buzzing. Other times I would just skip class and stay at the bar all day. I had a crush on my drinking buddy, Casey, and would stay and talk with him. Casey also chose to skip class. We lived close to each other, on the other side of campus, and he often drove me home. I didn't want to pay for the $150 parking pass and would walk the mile to school. When Casey's parents sent him to rehab, again, I would still be at the bar drinking. I studied there, wrote papers there, and usually ate there. The food was not half bad. I was most definitely a regular.

At TCC I had been a proactive student. I studied, got projects done early, attended class regularly, and participated in the large number of group projects. At TCU I was a lazy student. Apart from a few classes, like Statistics, I didn't need to study. The information was interesting, so it stuck in my head and there was very little research involved. I was a decent student, and finished in twenty-three months, but would probably have done better if I had put in more effort. I took mostly afternoon classes, which allowed me the time to write papers the morning they were due. I'd make an A or a high B and I figured I was fine; I didn't need to put in more effort. My motivation and reward circuit was confused, and I didn't see the need to change.

Most of the classes I took blended together. My one goal was to have my father see me walk across the stage, and I often took on more classes than I should have. My second goal was to get into law school. One of the best pieces of advice Captain Sheets had given me when I told him I wanted to be a lawyer was, "Take as many writing courses as you can." I had transferred in so many credits that I was already a senior, but I was required to take sixty more before TCU would allow me to graduate. I decided the best use of my time was to pursue two Bachelor of Arts degrees in subjects I thought would best prepare me for law school: sociology and philosophy.

I took classes like Bioethics, Law and Society, Religion and Anthropology, Religion and Literature, Argumentative Writing, and Social Problems. My favorite classes were Animals and Society and Sex, Society, and Ethics. My favorite professor was Dr. Thompson. Each semester I signed up for any class she was teaching, and I'm glad we've stayed in touch. All my classes were writing-heavy, with an abundance of reading. I learned how to form an argument and back it with logic. I loved learning new things and applying them to the political and social environment of the time. But the class I hated most was Advanced Issues in the Philosophy of Law and Economics.

It was a senior-level course, and I was worried that I didn't have enough background in econ. My advisor assured me I would do fine. It was a cross-listed course, and there would be econ students who had never taken a philosophy course, just as I had never taken an economics course. Boy, was he wrong. I felt behind the curve every day, and I struggled to comprehend the economics side of the class. My courses up to this point had felt more like conversations between professors and students. This course was just information thrown at us every day. I eventually caught on, but it was dry and difficult, not to mention infuriating. We looked at case after case of corporations using loopholes in laws and contracts to screw over the other party. I struggled daily and barely made a D, and I have a feeling they were being generous. Good thing it was an elective and I didn't have to repeat it.

At the end of the course the professor asked who had plans for law school after graduation and, to no one's surprise, everyone raised their hand. He then dropped the bomb that the way he had taught this course was how all law school courses were taught. I was left with an uncomfortable decision: continue with the idea of law school, knowing I would be set up for failure, or choose a different path. After a lifetime of struggle on difficult paths, I wanted no more of it. I was tired of struggling. I was exhausted and just wanted it easier. So I chose to forego law school. I decided to choose something easier, and I found public service to be rewarding and fulfilling.

CHAPTER 25

Shadow

It was at TCU that I gained more leadership skills. In my first semester, an Army student veteran named Matthew Smith was involved in a horrific wreck: motorcycle versus eighteen-wheeler. It was a miracle he survived, and he was likely going to be in the hospital for months. One of the student groups organized a blood drive, and the student veterans wanted to do something as well. Someone threw out the idea of making him a quilt, and I ran with it. I reached out to the student body, asking them to donate TCU t-shirts. The Title IX office donated patriotic fabric and thread. I cut up the t-shirts and fabric into four-inch squares for a twelve-inch nine block. When the blocks were all sewed together, the purple t-shirts spelled out TCU. There was enough donated material to make a second quilt. This one spelled TCU MOM. Once the quilt was pieced together, various student organizations came to the fourth-floor lounge in Scharbauer Hall to sign the quilts and fill them with messages of love and support. Some students chose to sew on a patch or draw a picture. When it was finished, the quilts were presented to Matthew's mother. There were tears and words of thanks. At the end of the semester, I was presented with the "Outstanding Student" award at the Multi-Cultural Affairs end-of-year banquet.

The next semester I was cornered by the president of the campus Student Veterans of America chapter. The chapter was in need of a secretary, and he thought I would be a good fit. He was graduating at the end of the semester, so Elyana, Quinn, and I ran for different offices. Quinn was named president, Elyana served as vice president, and I served as the public relations officer. Later on, I would hold the offices of vice president and president. My most daunting speaking engagement was at a Veterans Day Ceremony, with Mayor Betsy Price of Fort Worth in attendance.

While serving, we had the opportunity to attend various workshops and conferences held by the national organization. Student Veterans of America is headquartered in DC and is a voice for student veterans on more than 1500 campuses in all fifty states and several countries. They fight for us and were instrumental in the passage of the Forever GI Bill in 2017. Elyana and I drove up to one regional workshop in Kansas City, where we met with other students from the central U.S. Elyana, Quinn, and I all attended the national conference in San Antonio, along with four other TCU students. The conference is the largest gathering of post-9/11 veterans and students from all over the U.S. There are sessions and speakers on all sorts of topics, from updates on the GI Bill to panels on applying to graduate school.

While at TCU, I was stalked for the third time, the first being Mr. Colby with the help of the Mormon Church and the second a boy I dated in high school. This one was a graduate student from Bangladesh. He was studying mathematics and was a graduate teaching assistant. It was his first semester away from home, he lived in my apartment complex, and I was friendly to him. He invited me into his apartment to have delicious Bangladeshi food, and I invited him to my apartment so I could cook for him as well. I guess it was a cross-cultural misunderstanding, because he thought we were dating. I was very clear that we were not. But that did not stop him pursuing me. He had access to student records and looked up my schedule and would be waiting for me when my class ended. At one point, during a holiday break, he texted me asking if I was okay. He said he had noticed that my apartment lights had not been turned on in days, and he wanted to know if anything was wrong. After that I was terrified, and a friend slept on my couch for several days.

I cornered him on campus and shouted, "I am not your girlfriend!" I told him that if he did not quit stalking me I would report him to the university. I reminded him that losing his job and getting kicked out of TCU would mean his F-1 student visa would be revoked and he would be forced to leave the country. That did the trick.

I finished my two BAs and graduated on December 20, 2014, eight years after graduating from boot camp and a week to the day after my thirtieth birthday. My parents and siblings were there. The graduates were grouped by college and then alphabetically, and the College of Liberal Arts was up first. We got to the Cs, and soon I was on stage. Graduating seniors were allowed to take their finals early, so that they could receive their diplomas at the ceremony. Chancellor Boschini was handing out the diplomas and shaking the students' hands. When he picked up my two purple diploma covers, bundled together, he stopped me: "Young lady, do you know how hard it is for a student to get one degree, much less two?" We stood there for a few minutes as he grilled me on what I was going to be doing next and how proud he was of me. Mama said we held up the line for three minutes, him shaking my hand the whole time. He finally let go of my hand and the ceremony continued. Mama counted the number of students who received two diplomas; there were three of us.

None of the Colbys, aside from Guy, were at my graduation. I had invited some of them, but Mrs. Colby had died on my thirtieth birthday and Mr. Colby insisted on having the funeral on the day of my graduation. He asked me to be a pallbearer, and I refused. He didn't even ask me directly, but got my cousin Richard to ask me. If Mr. Colby had asked me directly, I would have told him to go to hell. About a year before, I had told them that I would allow them in my life only if they renounced Baren, and they had refused. I saw them once, when Mrs. Colby was in the hospital. Richard had taken me, knowing how hard it was going to be. Mr. Colby refused to give us the room and instead was showing off photos of his grandkids to the nurse. He made sure to emphasize how proud he was of Baren and his newest children. He passed his wallet to her, directly in front of my face; it was open to a photo of Baren with his new wife and children. Everyone was all grins for the camera. I wanted to punch him in the face and rip his throat out. Instead, Richard and I quickly left.

Even though I told them I didn't want to be part of their lives or have them in mine, Mr. Colby chose to continue harassing me with phone calls, emails, and letters. The night before my thirtieth birthday, I saw I had another birthday card from them, and I threw it across the room. No one was there but still I shouted, "When will I fucking be free of them?" The next morning, I awoke to a phone call saying that Mrs. Colby had died. I felt shock, then guilt. I blamed myself for saying what I did and thought God was punishing me by ensuring our lives will forever be tied together. Every birthday, I am reminded of her death.

Part of me wanted to go to the funeral, and I might have, had Mr. Colby not scheduled it on the day of my graduation. Maybe it was a good thing I had an excuse to not go, as Baren was there. He had been given special permission by his parole officer to leave Idaho, and if I had been forced to interact with him, I would have gone to jail for attempted murder. Richard and his wife Stephanie made a short appearance at my party, on their way from the funeral to the graveside. But they were the only Colbys to make an appearance.

Today I have forgiven my grandmother for the role she played in the abuse. I don't have any proof, but I have a feeling she was not complicit in any of the horrors subjected on her children and grandchildren. I truly believe she was trapped in an abusive marriage, since divorce in the Mormon church is nearly impossible and a divorcee risks being excommunicated. But in 2014, I still held on to my anger, contempt, and hostility.

CHAPTER 26

In the Stars

After graduation I stayed in Fort Worth for a few months, attending interview after interview. Finally, I was hired by Texas State Technical College and moved to Marshall, Texas. My car was in terrible shape, and I was down to my last twenty dollars. I "pawned" a box of my most prized possessions to Mama for two hundred dollars. I hated asking for money from anyone, so I figured this way I wasn't asking, just borrowing. I didn't need to worry about rent as my Nanny and Papa, my mother's parents, lived an hour away and said I could crash with them until I started getting paid and could rent a place. The air conditioning in my car had gone out, and it was rather warm in Texas in March. I had to drive with the windows down and carried a gallon of water with me.

Marshall is off Interstate 20, and the closest big city is Shreveport, Louisiana. If you took the entire population of Marshall and put them in the Amon G. Carter Stadium at TCU, it would only be half full. I was hired to be the veteran certifier, recruiter, adviser, and whatever other hat the school threw at me. I knew no one in Marshall and struggled to make friends, much less find someone to date. There were no bars or activities for adults. The only social activities revolved around children or church, and I had neither. Mama suggested I go to Mass to meet someone, but I didn't think hoping to meet a man was an appropriate reason to go to church. The only men I interacted with were either coworkers or students, and I wasn't going to pursue either category.

Instead I signed up for online dating, which sucked. So many of the men were losers, and the dates were terrible. A student had run across my profile and had the nerve to bring it up. He had "liked" the profile and had the delusional idea that he stood a chance. By July 2015, I had come to peace with the idea of staying single and went to take down the profile. I saw I had a message from a new match and decided to read it. It was a sweet message, not raunchy like so many others. I looked at his profile and he seemed very nice. He was a few years older than me, a childless widower, and worked for the Texas Department of Criminal Justice. Much better than other matches, who had been guests of TDCJ. He had chosen online dating because everyone in Carthage was related to his late wife.

I agreed to go on a date with Sean, and we hit it off. Our first date was at the Jalapeno Tree, followed by a movie. Is it any surprise  we saw Max, a movie about a Marine bomb-detecting dog? After the movie we walked around the downtown square. Neither of us wanted the date to end. He told me about his late wife's brain cancer, and I told him about my dad's kidney cancer. We talked religion, and I teased him about being a Baptist drinking a beer. We talked about our families and our jobs. He was working Coffield Unit, a maximum-security men's prison. His shifts were four days on, four days off, and he stayed in officers' quarters while on shift.

We continued to date, and eight months later I moved in with him. I loved the house I was renting, a shotgun-style three-bedroom with a galley kitchen a five-minute drive to work, but the rent was $600 a month and Sean's was $300 a month on his parents' land. So I moved into his trailer and settled down for life in the country, forty minutes from work. I had wanted to start an online post-baccalaureate teaching program, but there was no internet service out there; there still isn't. There was nothing to do, so I took up woodworking. Sean was gone every four days and I traveled a lot for work, so Sean's mom would look after our cats, Miles and Bruce, when we were both away.

Life was going well. I was dating a man I adored and who adored me. I had bought my first brand-new car and was thrilled to not have to worry about it breaking down. I made enough money to not only pay all my bills, but to play around with as well. For our first anniversary we decided to take a road trip to New Orleans, and we couldn't wait to explore the city. But before we could go, we got a call from Mama. Dad had taken a turn for the worse, and the doctors didn't think he would make it to the end of the summer. Mama wanted to have one last family vacation at Disney World. It was Sarah's twenty-first birthday and Karen's twenty-eighth, and it would be a present to them. Mama thought it would be nice for everyone to come. Karen, Steven, and the kids booked their flights, and Steve shortened his yoga trip to Costa Rica. Sean and I decided to still spend a few days in New Orleans but would make it a longer road trip. We also went to Knoxville so Brandy and Paul could meet Sean. They had been married for five years at this point and had moved to Knoxville for graduate school.

While visiting them we went into the Smokey Mountains. The height of the mountains made me nervous, and the higher we went the more I freaked out. Twice I made Sean pull over to a protected shoulder so I could get my bearings. Each time I implored him to slow down. They suggested I close my eyes, but that made it worse. The plan had been to make it to Clingmans Dome, but I was having none of it. I saw a sign that said it was another four miles to the overlook, and I made Sean pull over a third time. This shoulder had a little creek to wade in, and I told Sean he could go ahead and take pictures and I would stay here. Brandy said she had seen it many times before and would stay with me. As Sean drove off Brandy commented, "I think he's the one."

"Oh, why?"

"Because we're on the side of a mountain with no cell service, and you just let him drive off with your car and wallet."

I laughed but I trusted him to come back, which he did.

From Knoxville we drove across the Carolinas to the sea. Sean had never seen the Atlantic Ocean. It was the first time I had been back to South Carolina, and we viewed Parris Island and the Beaufort River. I had forgotten how beautiful the area was and remembered back to when I could see the sailboats from the beach during PT. Then we drove down to Orlando and arrived late at night. Mama had gotten us suites at her timeshare.

Disney World was a wonderful trip. We had rented Dad a wheelchair, and Mama expected him to stay only a few hours. He stayed five and enjoyed the parade. We all returned back to our homes, and Dad's health continued to decline. All of his siblings, plus his parents, came for a final visit – the last time all ten of them were in one place. As he got worse I talked my boss into letting me work out of the Red Oak campus, which was outside Dallas and only thirty miles from my parents' house. I wanted to be closer to help Mama. He agreed, as long as I returned to Marshall once a week. Dad's parents, Popo Pat and Popo Tony, came down. Another of Dad's brothers,  Uncle Mark, came down from Michigan. Steve would come over most nights to help, and we would play Uno with Dad. It broke my heart when Dad stopped being able to recognize the colors, and we always pretended he was right.

In the end the cancer had spread all the way to his brain, and he began hallucinating. He weighed less than ninety pounds, and we begged him to eat. He might have lost his faculties, but he kept his sense of humor. One morning, as I was getting ready for work, I heard Mama on the baby monitor, imploring him to eat something.

"Paul, I will make anything, just please tell me what you would want. What is your favorite thing to eat?"

"Pussy," he replied.

He wanted to die at home, and Mama had set up at-home hospice. But the nurse came only twice a week for thirty minutes, and it got to be too much. Mama had been with him all day, with no one there to help. She needed some medication for him, and everyone else was at work. She called the home health care line, and the person on the other end told her what to get from the pharmacy. When Mama protested, saying he couldn't be left alone, she was met with a callous response: "Don't you have someone to call?" Mama thought to herself, "Well, I just did."

A friend was able to help, but the product the customer service person said to get was wrong; it was the product a doctor would give for someone about to have a colonoscopy. Dad was too weak to move and would stand on Mama's feet with his arms around her neck, like a little girl at her first daddy-daughter dance.

One of these nights I was sleeping on the couch, and Mama woke me up asking for my help; there had been an accident in the middle of the night, and she needed my help cleaning him up. It was just too much, and she made the decision to put him in a hospice facility. A day after he entered the facility, he slipped into a coma.

At 2:00 a.m. the nurse told Mama it was the end, and that she should call the family. All of the local aunts and uncles and cousins showed up. Sean, Sarah, and I drove up there. Uncle Mark had gone back to Michigan, so we called him to give his goodbyes over the phone. Out-of-town family members began making their travel arrangements.

But Dad made it through the night and the next day. It was as if he had heard the nurse and wanted to defy her. The family all stayed by his bedside, napping on the couches in the waiting room and taking turns talking to Dad. Steve made rounds to get food for the family, and we all waited on the inevitable. By 8:00 p.m. Mama sent us all home, promising to keep us updated. I tried sleeping, knowing the phone call would come soon. I got up that morning and called Mama. He was still with us, so I decided to go into work.

I stopped by a local donut shop for kolaches and coffee. I had gotten a few blocks down the road when Mama called again. He was gone. It was August 18, 2016. He was fifty-nine years old. I swung back to pick up Sean and Sarah. I was too numb to cry and sat quietly in a chair in the corner of the room while the staff prepared Dad's body to be taken away. Uncle James touched my shoulder and told me I didn't have to stay in the room. I looked up at him as if he were speaking French and didn't move. When I went back to my parents' house I saw the uneaten kolache and the coffee cup. They had long since gone cold, but I couldn't bring myself to throw them away. They belonged in the before, and I was now in the after. I wanted to hold on to the before as long as I could.

The next few days were a blur of people, food, and sympathy. Friends from all over came to town, including Mama's best friend Aunt Karen. She stayed with us the longest. I went with Mama to pick out a coffin and to discuss funeral arrangements. She and Dad had discussed all his wishes. Some Mama was going to honor, others she vetoed. He had wanted certain flowers and picked his pallbearers. He asked a family friend to officiate and picked out the scripture. She honored these. He also wanted his cell phone to be placed in the casket and have ring tones such as "I Will Survive" and "The Bitch is

Back." He wanted people to call him during the Mass. Mama quickly vetoed these, saying Popo Pat would have a heart attack.

Catholic wakes are open casket, but the funeral is closed casket. Uncle Mark's family couldn't make it to the wake. Neither could Karen. Mama didn't want five-year-old Kolbe to miss her first day of Kindergarten and told Karen to come the next morning. Because of this I insisted on a second, private viewing the morning of the funeral so that they could say goodbye. It was at the wake that I started to lose it. I started to tear up, and Deacon Charles pulled me aside and told me not to cry. He said I needed to be strong for my Mama and my siblings. I was furious. How dare he tell me I could not openly mourn my father!

Karen and the kids came in during the private viewing, and everyone started crying again. Kolbe was confused and asked Mama why she was sad. Mama explained that she was sad because we were saying goodbye to her grandpa. She told Kolbe that he had died. Mama picked her up so she could see him in the casket. Kolbe asked if he was going to wake up and was upset when Mama said no.

The morning of the funeral came, and I wanted to escape. But I gave the eulogy and was fine until I saw my Aunt Alicia crying, and I sobbed in front of everyone as I tried to say the last line. We took the limo to the gravesite, and I tried focusing on breathing rather than screaming. We were milling about, waiting on the priest, when Kolbe said loudly that she wanted to say something. Everyone got quiet, and Mama picked her up. She pointed at the casket and announced: "My grandpa died, and we put him in that box."

There was nervous silence, then Mama laughed and said, "You are right. And he would have loved that you told that joke."

As the year went on, it became easier to accept my dad's death. We had our first Thanksgiving, my first birthday, and our first Christmas without him. Our year of firsts was hard, but we survived through the morose celebrations. Until New Year's Eve. I panicked. I wanted to stop time so that 2017 never came. I didn't want to enter a year in which Dad didn't exist.

CHAPTER 27

THE GOOD ONES

By the end of 2016 I was fed up with living in the country and longed for the city. I told Sean I was going to be applying for other jobs. He supported me but asked two things: Don't leave Texas, and don't pick Houston. I agreed. Neither of us liked Houston. I applied to jobs in Austin, Fort Worth, San Antonio, and Dallas. I was granted a few interviews, and in mid-December I received an offer from the Texas Veterans Commission in Austin. Sean most definitely wanted to join me, as he was originally from San Marcos, a short drive south of the city, and he missed home. It took a year for his transfer to go through, so he was still traveling to Tennessee Colony every four days. I spent that alone time exploring our new city. We had a group of friends already here, as we had come down often for parties. Our friends were happy to show us around and take us to their favorite places. Austin has a good foodie scene and many outdoor activities. The Hill Country has several rivers, and Sean was determined to make me a river rat. That first summer he took me to his favorite river, the San Marcos, and persuaded me to float it. The San Marcos comes off Spring Lake and is crystal clear. Spring Lake is protected due to the Austin Blind Salamanders and is so clear you can see thirty feet down to the fault line. It is where the Gulf Coast region ends and the Hill Country begins, and you can see the water rushing up from the Edward Aquifer. It makes the sand look like it's boiling. Sean got his scientific diving license there when he was a teenager and was responsible for keeping the lake floor clean.

The week before we closed on our new house in Austin, Sean proposed. I later learned that he had told my dad a year earlier that he was going to ask me to marry him. Dad beamed and was pleased to know I would be okay.

Planning the wedding took eighteen months, and we planned the wedding of our dreams. However, several fears turned my stomach into knots and kept me up at night. I worried that Mr. Colby would show up, and that Guy would cause a scene. Guy had behaved badly at Karen's wedding in 2010, mad that he didn't get to walk her down the aisle or get the Daddy/Daughter dance, and had left, loudly, during the toasts. Karen wrote him off after that.

The worries got worse when Mr. Colby sent me the gift. He had seen the wedding invitation on my Uncle Christopher's fridge, with the password to our wedding website and, consequently, our address. There was going to be an open bar, and I worried Guy would get too drunk and cause a scene. I worried about seating arrangements and where to put him. I was being walked down the aisle by my godfather, my Uncle Sam, and he would get the Daddy/Daughter dance in memory of my dad. I had to have the difficult conversation with Guy that he wasn't being given this honor. He seemed to take it well, but I worried that he would not be okay once he had alcohol in his system.

As the day approached, I would get sick spinning scenarios. I contemplated hiring plainclothes officers. Instead I asked several larger male friends to keep an eye out and remove him if it got bad. They also needed to keep an eye out for Mr. Colby. Thankfully my fears were not realized, and Sean and I were married without any Colby drama.

No One Leaves Unscathed

CHAPTER 28

Mean!

A few months after our wedding, we found out that Sean couldn't have children. We were trying to come to terms with this devastating news, and trying to decide between using a sperm donor or adoption, when I realized my old friend Arthur had moved to Austin. We needed some happiness to take our minds off our troubles, so I reached out to see if he wanted to get dinner sometime. Sean couldn't make it due to work, so I went alone to the swanky taco shop Arthur suggested.

He was charming and interested in what I had to say. We quickly became close friends, and the three of us started hanging out nearly every weekend. We checked out different foodie locales and hung out on the river on the hot Hill Country summer days. I started drinking heavily to keep up with him. At first I made excuses to Sean for my drinking, or when Arthur got trashed and broke something in our house. Neither of us wanted him to drink and drive, so we started letting him crash in our guest room. He would rant and rave about how good my cooking was, that I needed to post about it on Instagram. I finally gave in, and I started getting followers in the Austin foodie scene. When I started getting invitations to influencer events, Arthur proclaimed that Instagram was stupid and overrated. He would try to convince me to cancel on them because "They aren't your real friends."

Even as more and more red flags popped up, I dismissed them as one-off things due to Arthur's drinking and untreated PTSD. He had served on a submarine, and he would get drunk and cry on my shoulder about how he felt like he couldn't breathe when the sub was underwater. I saw him as broken and thought I could help. But the more I tried to help, the worse things got. His drinking worsened and he lashed out. If I stood up for myself, he would erupt in a violent tantrum and I would end up with a bruise. The worse Arthur treated me, the harder I tried to help him get better. I didn't want to let him down, because of how many people had left him behind. I convinced myself that if I could help him stop drinking, he would be better. I told myself he was a nice guy deep down. But the cycle kept repeating, and at the end of the day I would cry. Somewhere along the way he stopped being charming, but I had become too involved.

Arthur blamed me and Sean for his own behavior. He broke our La-Z-Boys on New Year's Eve 2019 because he was so drunk that he passed out standing up, then blamed me for placing them in the middle of the room. He tried pushing me down the stairs that night, despite knowing I was pregnant. Sean and I had decided to use a sperm donor, and the artificial insemination had been successful. We were thrilled to be parents and had dipped into our savings to pay for the treatments. Arthur knew how long and hard we had tried to become pregnant. A few days after New Year's Eve, I lost the baby.

He ripped shelves off my wall because he couldn't walk straight and complained that they were in his way. Every time I opened my mouth he called me a crazy liberal, and when I pointed out that he had said the same thing five minutes earlier, he would grab my arms so hard I had bruises the next day. If I complained that he hurt me, he told me I needed to "Marine up" and stop being a pussy. Anything that was mine had to be his: weed, soda, food, friends, alcohol, prescription meds, my own body.

In January 2020 we were kicked out of a Tool concert because Arthur was so trashed that he started fights. I didn't have a drop of alcohol that night, because we had done another fertility treatment and there was a chance I was pregnant again. I was mortified. As we were leaving, Arthur nearly fell down a flight of stairs. I had to calm him down by saying he was saving me money by making us leave early, because the Uber would be cheaper. Down in the lobby he realized he had lost his phone and I had to go back up, past all the people who had witnessed his behavior. Sure enough it was under his seat, and I had to ask the two guys he had tried to fight to hand it to me. I could not look them in the eye. As I walked back down, I felt empathy for what Mama had gone through in public with Guy. When I called Arthur the next day to talk about his behavior, he started screaming at me and hung up.

Yet I kept coming back for more. When women broke up with him, he threw me against walls and demanded to know why no woman would ever love him. By the time the pandemic started, we couldn't get rid of him. He came over every Saturday and stayed for days. I told Sean it was because he had no family in Austin and needed to get out of his tiny apartment. If I told Arthur I needed to do laundry or dishes, he'd bitch and moan about how he came over to spend time with us. In the next breath, he'd call our house fucking disgusting because there were dirty dishes and broken furniture. He stole medications and expensive wines and lied about it, even if we caught him in the act.

Any time I tried to put some distance between us by not calling or texting him, he'd draw me back in by saying he was going to jump off his fifth-floor balcony. I had lost veteran friends to suicide and took the threat seriously. I would drop whatever I was doing and go to his apartment and sleep on the couch. If I offered to call in a mental health check, he would scream that if I ever called the cops on him, he would never forgive me.

I was in an abusive, toxic friendship with an addict who loved turning my world upside down. I would like to say that when he stuck his penis in my face and demanded a blow job, I ended our friendship then and there. But I didn't. I was at his apartment watching a movie. He had gotten a dog, Mae, a few months before, and she was best friends with my four-year-old pit bull, Greyson. I had started going over there for playdates. I told him it was because I liked being closer to the trails, and Grey and I would hit them before we came over. The reality was that Sean didn't want Arthur in our house anymore. I was sitting on his couch while the dogs played on the floor, and I heard him come out of the bathroom behind me. I turned to ask what he wanted to order for dinner. Before I could react, he grabbed my head and demanded a blow job. I jumped up and grabbed my dog to leave.

I was sober, so I knew there was no reason I should feel guilty for his behavior, but I did. The whole drive home I wracked my brain, trying to figure out where he could have mixed up my behavior to think I would do such a thing. I decided not to tell Sean yet. The next morning, I called Arthur to confront him. He went off on me, saying it was all a joke, that he was obviously not sexually attracted to me. I was furious. But I chose not to push the issue further, or tell Sean, because we were days away from going to Colorado for our anniversary, and Arthur was housesitting for us for free. I bit my tongue and told myself that I would end our friendship when we got home.

This was just after election night 2020, and some close family weren't speaking to me. I was incredibly lonely. I had made a tongue-in-cheek post about how the best thing about election night was that I would no longer have to see the awful John Cornyn ads. Cornyn was running for reelection to his U.S. Senate seat against MJ Hegar, a popular local woman who was an Air Force veteran. She was a pilot and had been the lead plaintiff who had sued the federal government over the Combat Exclusion Policy in 2012. While the lawsuit had failed, the policy had been repealed in 2013. From that moment on women could be in combat fields such as infantry, as fighter pilots, and doing reconnaissance. In 2021 a sailor became the first woman Naval Special Forces combat-craft crewman, operating the boats that transport the SEALs. And of the eighteen women who had tried out to be a SWCC or a SEAL, this sailor was the first to pass. All of us can thank MJ Hegar for her trailblazing badassery.

In order to get the "woman vote," Cornyn had run ads trying to take Hegar down a peg. One of the ways he did this was to talk about a bill he and several colleagues had authored to deal with the backlog of rape test kits. Yes, this was an important bill. And yes, it had been long due to pass. But to make himself seem like a hero, Cornyn had women tell their rape stories in his ads. At the time I was not dealing well with my assaults, and these ads were incredibly triggering. I felt he was running them only because he was running against a strong woman.

My post simply said, "I am glad we no longer have to see his exploitative ads." And then I went to work and didn't get back on Facebook until 4:00 p.m., when I was bombarded with a shit show. One aunt commented that she was proud she had voted straight Republican and wanted Trump to win. A friend jumped on her, pointing out that there was no reason to bring Trump into the conversation, when the post had been about a senator's advertising. This started a back-and-forth argument where her children jumped in and other friends backed each other. At one point the word "cunt" was thrown out.

Several people were tagging me, saying I needed to respond to the things my friends were saying. I had private messages from people, yelling at me for not defending them. One cousin kept trying to taunt me, saying that liberals all claim to want to talk but then never do. A friend pointed out that liberals had been talking all along, and by the morning of the election they were tired. I got a phone call from my mother telling me I needed to apologize to my aunt. Apparently, my silence meant I agreed with my friend. I laughed and told her I was not going to apologize for something a grown adult had done; I was tired of apologizing for other people's behavior. By the end of the night people were posting the "eating popcorn" meme. That aunt still does not speak to me and is waiting on an apology that will never come. It would have been funny if I had been in a better place mental health-wise, but I was tired. From all of this, I was not speaking to many of my own family, and Arthur's abuse made it even more isolating.

We got home from Colorado on Sunday, and Arthur had completely trashed our house. An unknown sticky red sauce was spilled all over the kitchen counter. There was a convenience store's worth of empty beer bottles in every trash can and recycling can and on every countertop. Nice Tupperware had been thrown away in the large outdoor trash can. Our cat's water fountain was bone dry. There was a ring of dried vomit in our tub and on the shower curtain, broken glass downstairs, and dog pee upstairs. But it was 11:30 p.m. and I was tired. We had spent the week hiking and playing in the snow, and I wanted to hold on to the memories of the week a little longer before I called Arthur.

I had worked out in my head the exact words, to try to avoid setting him off. I was wrong. At 2:00 p.m. on Sunday, November 15, 2020 I called him, mostly to ask if he would come clean up the ring of vomit in the tub. He immediately started screaming at me that we had left the house "fucking disgusting," then hung up on me and texted that he was "so fucking angry" at us. The texts continued, blaming us for asking him to housesit despite knowing he had issues about not sleeping in his own bed. He claimed he was so depressed about that that he got drunk and blacked out, and that he hadn't realized he had thrown up in the tub until the next morning when it was clogged. He claimed Sean and I turned everything into a big deal and only ever focused on the negatives, and if we had left his house in that condition, he would have just cleaned it up and laughed about it later with us.

I responded:

You come over every week, trash our house, break our shit, and then act like I am the bad guy for being upset. It is not okay to behave the way you do at people's houses. But I let it slide because our dogs get along so well. It is not okay to act like I am the bad guy for being upset when I have every right to be. You are being manipulative and a jerk. You want to throw a temper tantrum because I called you out on your crap? Go ahead. I hope you find peace and are able to get past your trauma that causes you to be a raging alcoholic. But I am done being your punching bag.

Arthur responded by blocking me on Facebook and Instagram. I couldn't understand what I had done to deserve such treatment from a friend. But I have accepted this type of treatment from abusers and narcissists my entire life. It happened when I was a child, again when I was a teenager, again in the Marines, and again in my thirties.

CHAPTER 29

SOFT DARK NOTHING

Brandy's swearing brought me back to the present. "Wow! See, you have to finish this story. It deserves to be told. I just have one question: Is Guy still a part of your life?"

"No. The last time we spoke on the phone was when I called him to tell him I was pregnant. He was so callous and replied, 'Well, it's about time.' When I reminded him that Sean couldn't have children, he responded, "Well, of course he can't have children. He's a man.' He was so sarcastic, and it hurt."

"I am so sorry," said Brandy. "What did he say when you lost the baby?"

"I texted him and he didn't respond." I teared up, remembering how it had stung, and my hand instinctively went to my stomach. "There really wasn't one last straw, but a series of them. In September 2020, when Sean and I had Covid, he got onto me for not keeping him in the loop. He had the nerve to tell me that he is my father and deserves to be notified when I am sick."

Brandy laughed derisively. "Your husband was in the hospital in the early months of the pandemic, and he chose then to demand his fatherly respect."

"Yes. I was not as sick as Sean, but I was still exhausted. I would wake up, call Sean's doctor, notify our mothers, and go back to sleep. The doctors wanted to intubate Sean, but we refused. Back then, intubation was tantamount to a death sentence."

"I remember. You said there were other straws?"

"The longer the pandemic got, the longer his drunk and paranoid text messages got. They would come in the middle of the night, and I would dread reading them. Once he said he could beat Ted Cruz in a debate. Another said he was going to start his own political party. And then another said society was out to get him and the government was tracking his text messages. He was also texting Steve and Mama random rants about Trump."

Brandy stifled laughter. "I am sorry, it isn't funny."

"We think the four decades of drinking daily had finally rotted his brain. We are seriously surprised he hasn't died of cirrhosis. I know that sounds awful, but it is the truth. Karen and I have prepared ourselves for the call to say he's drunk himself to death. We have questioned who will pay for the funeral, since I know he is leaving us with nothing but debt. Back in April I sent him a paragraphs-long text message that explained why I was blocking his number and imploring him to not reach out anymore."

Brandy was silent for a long moment. "This is a terrible position to be in, but I understand. Maybe you can try again after the book is published."

"I doubt it. This book will be the thing that severs our relationship for good. Part of me feels guilty. But another part of me wants to finally close my heart to him. I have given him chance after chance after chance, and he lets me down every time. I don't doubt that he loved me at one point, but he always lets me down and always chooses alcohol."

Brandy and I had been on the phone for fourteen hours, and we were both tired. We had gone through our day, taking care of dogs and children, all while I told her every story I wanted to include in my book. It was dark outside, and we both needed rest. She had fed her son dinner and needed to put him to bed. She thanked me for trusting her with my story and said she couldn't wait to read it. I thanked her for listening to me all day. I hung up the phone and was instantly aware of the deafening silence. I ran my hands through my greasy hair and was once again lost in my thoughts. The voices started again, and they were screaming.

It's easy to look back and see the roads I didn't take, the what-ifs. What if I had studied harder at DLI? What if I hadn't trusted the wrong people? What if I had moved to Hawaii with Charlie? What if I had gone to law school? What if I had not struggled with weight? What if I had majored in something different? What if I had never gone into the Marines?

I have no doubt that, had I not been assaulted during my first few months in the Marines, I would not have dipped into depression and alcoholism and would have done better at DLI. I would have been the linguist that I set out to be and would have built a strong career in intelligence. If I hadn't been bullied for weight and had been given access to a proper nutritionist, I would likely still be in the Marines as I write this – or instead of writing this – and getting ready to retire. If I had chosen Hawaii, Charlie and I would have gotten married. If I had gone to law school, I would be working on the civil rights issues of our time.

If I had had a different NCO and captain, I would have made a different choice. I would have kept my weight down and stayed in shape. I would have stayed in. If I had been sent to the fleet, I would likely have closed out my twenty years in 2026. I can see that career, and I am nostalgic for lost days. I have friends who have retired from the Marines, and I look at their careers with jealousy. But then I come back to reality, and I'm happy where I am. My career became different than I planned. My career in education led me to fabulous people. I met so many folks at Texas Christian University that I'm still in touch with. My mentors, best friends, and bosses came directly from the lessons I learned at TCU. But there's still truth in saying that I despised my bosses at the JRB. I have an answer for every one of these ifs.

Up to this point I have been pleased with the paths I chose for myself. Each one led to opportunities I would otherwise have missed. Joining the Marines gave me access to an education. Failing my DLPT led me to Charlie and the legal shop. The legal shop led me to a desire to give a voice to the voiceless. The desire to help led me to choose TCU, a school I knew would give me the education I needed, over Hawaii and a future as a Navy wife. TCU led me away from law school but introduced me to mentors like April Brown and Ethan Casey. I had the opportunity to share my story, which led me to write this memoir. The choice to work with veterans in higher education led me to a small town in northeast Texas where I met my husband, Sean Lynch. Each one of my what-ifs played out exactly as it should have, to make me the person I am today. Looking back may be a fun exercise, but nowhere along the way did I go wrong.

While I survived each time, a lifetime of survival was exhausting. I was tired of the never-ending fight. It seemed so many people had an easier life, and I found it unfair. This was not how it was supposed to be. I wasn't supposed to learn about rape at the age of six. I wasn't supposed to have a hard time in the Marine Corps.

Having spent all day on the phone, I had a general idea of how to tell my story, and I sat in front of my computer. As I tried to type, my hands shook, and I asked myself when was the last time I had eaten anything. After a paragraph I closed my laptop, too tired to type. I took an orange from the table and ate it standing in my kitchen. The boys were staring at me, and I wondered how long it had been since I had fed them. I gave them food, feeling guilty. I was failing everyone and worried I was killing my dogs. They would be better off without me. They all would.

I was so tired and wanted it all to be over. I shut myself in the bathroom, crying. Everything hurt, and a lifetime of pain washed over me. And then, suddenly, I stopped crying. The answer to my pain was clear. Through the clearing I saw moments in my life when I had been happy, and I wanted to get back to those. I had done so many things with my life, and I was okay if it all ended here. I had climbed mountains, kayaked oceans, and traveled the world. I had lived in another country and made friends all over the United States. I had loved deeply and been loved in return. I had three great love stories, while some are lucky to have one. I had completed in my thirty-six years more than others complete in eighty, and I was okay with not seeing thirty-seven.

I was tired of fighting with myself and the world and viewed my choice as logical. Unlike my life, this would be painless. I popped each of the sleeping pills out of its foil, and with each one I became calmer. My hands had stopped shaking. I was okay. The voices had gone silent. Once I had the entire package out, I swallowed them all with a swig of water. I sat there on the floor. I decided that I needed to hear Mama's voice one more time. I got her voicemail and was sad. I decided to leave a message but don't remember what I said. As I got more sleepy, I was hit with one thought: I would never be a mom. Maybe that was for the best, given how this was ending. Maybe I would have a chance in the next life. My breathing got shallower and I closed my eyes, comfortable with the thought that they were not going to open again. I slumped against the wall.

EPILOGUE

A Soft Place to Land

The universe tests you in all ways, at all times, and it never ends until you're dead.

That is a weirdly bleak statement, but it helps me in my darkest moments, when all feels lost. I have been to the brink of despair and felt that suicide might be the only answer. I have lain in bed and thought of the various ways I could die and been uncomfortably okay with the idea.

The scariest part was the realization that a part of me was right. Death is, at times, the answer to the question, "How do I get out of this?"

How do I get out of a financial black hole?

How do I get out of going to war again?

How do I get out of this crime I committed?

How do I get out of being honest with my spouse that I've fucked up our lives?

How do I get out of ever seeing my boss again?

How do I get out of another family function?

How do I get out of admitting to my parents that I haven't gone to class in three months?

How do I get out of being a bad mother?

I have felt scarily comfortable with the answer to these questions being death. I would feel it and know it and be okay with it. Each time, I have gone to the brink of despair, looked death in the eye, and said no, until I didn't. And each time, when the answer did appear for me, it was something else, until it wasn't. I am obviously not dead; Sean found me in time. It is an odd thing to verbalize, but that is what the depression side of a mood disorder feels like, and it sucks. It sucks even more that I can't help the depression. It's a chemical imbalance in my brain that causes me to feel things differently than others do. There is a difference between enduring a period of depression and having schizoaffective disorder. There is also absolutely nothing wrong with it. It is a medical diagnosis that affects many people but is written off as a joke by people who lack empathy.

The key moments that made up my childhood could be summed up as how I was born, how I learned, and how I survived. I was born into poverty and religion, I learned strength from my mother, and I survived by keeping to myself. These moments set the groundwork for why I ran away from college at twenty-one to join the Marines. During a time of war.

Those who meet me now seem shocked when I tell them I was in the Marines, and I don't blame them. I am a highly educated theist, an outspoken pacifist, and a defender of the importance of early childhood education. I've partied with nudists, smoked pot with artists and adventurers, and support moderate gun restriction. I will openly talk with my opposites on religion, human rights, and education, and I admire professors over rock stars. Give me a conversation with a music professor who moonlights as a concert blues performer, or a prominent doctor who mountain climbs for fun and donates free surgeries to the needy, any day of the week. I look to teaching as the greatest life skill to attain. Some teach from knowledge; some teach from experience. The best teachers teach from both.

The people in my early life who taught me were my family, just as much as teachers in school. I learned strength, love, curiosity, and forgiveness from the best of them. I learned hate, lying, and distrust from the sickest of them. But the best skill of all was how to fight. I could fight with my words as well as with my fists. I also knew that surviving by being silent was sometimes the best action. I was silent so many times when I should have been screaming, and I screamed when I should have been silent. I was silent about the abuse in my grandparents' house, and I threw violent temper tantrums at Six Flags. The lessons we learn in childhood often need to be unlearned in adulthood, and the wiring needs to be remapped.

My attempt at life is to learn how to stop using my words to hurt people and instead use them to help people. I am good at speaking kindly to strangers, but I have a sharp tongue when it's needed. One of my best friends says I'm the epitome of not putting up with anyone else's shit. I can cut someone off for an indiscretion and never look back. But I am also awful at judging character. The problem with rose-colored glasses is that it's hard to see the stop signs until you're teetering on a cliff.

I'm learning to be cautious rather than jumping all in. I'm learning to listen for clues in a person's behavior, and not to play all my cards until they're needed. I can be open and honest with my closest friends, but there are layers of information that other people get to know. I vet everyone on Facebook, and I'm careful which details I give out on Instagram. I don't often post in real time, so as to prevent stalkers from knowing everything. If that sounds paranoid, I have been stalked three times.

All of these red flags and stop signs we're supposed to notice right away get muddied when you're taught from age six that you're not in control of what happens to your body. When that basic form of trust is eroded between a child and her caregiver, it blurs our behavior into adulthood. You learn either to give everything away, all the time, to everyone, or to never trust a single person ever. The more logical option is therapy, but that takes time, and many are not able to devote their time to mental health. Some cannot afford it, some replace therapy with religion, others doubt the efficacy. For many it's cheaper to seek out dealers or bartenders, finding solace in their oblivion.

If, post-pandemic, you doubt whether public health care is important, just search "veterans support programs in my area." You will find either nothing or an overabundance. Both issues are due to the privatization of the VA system and the repeated lack of proper funding. If you still doubt it, talk to a veteran who has fallen through the cracks. If you don't know any veterans, google "Clay Hunt Act" and listen to Clay Hunt's mother plead with Congress to help change the VA system that killed her son.

Survivors of military sexual assault feel doubly betrayed, because of how long it took for change to happen for us. Women and men who were abused in service are less likely to report abuse than to go to sick hall for pneumonia. Let that sit for a moment. I was twenty-three and in California. I had pneumonia so bad that the detachment master gunnery sergeant had to threaten me with a reduction in rank just to get me to admit I was sick and go to sick hall. I went, reluctantly. But I wasn't going to open my mouth about the sexual abuse and exploitation of women and gay Marines in his unit. It took me ten years to open up about my own abuse, and it devastated me to discover that other women had had the exact same abusers I did.

I have struggled with how much or how little to write about. It has taken me two years to write my story. Here's a hint: Don't do it alone. Make sure you have someone to talk to and a therapist during the writing project. If you can't afford a therapist, one can be provided to you by a nonprofit organization. Please don't push yourself to the extremes of memory recollection without seeking mental health help. Don't do what I did and be signed into a mental health ward by a judge. For nine days. The day before your birthday. Thirteen days before Christmas.

I have been joking that the day I nearly died was the coldest day in hell, but really my entire life has been teetering between heaven and hell. For thirty years I've tiptoed that line, never really living. I added more and more fears, and bottled up every negative emotion, until it nearly killed me. But I woke up at age thirty-seven and spent another week getting better in a controlled hospital setting. I made friends and rediscovered art. I cried, a lot, but mostly laughed. And I listened.

I listened to a mother who had survived a recent suicide attempt, who felt guilty that her daughters had almost been the ones to find her. I listened to a philomath who looked eerily like "white Jesus." I listened to mothers and fathers who had fallen off the wagon and just wanted to go home for Christmas for their little kids. I shared colors with a severely autistic adult, and I ate with artists. I honestly felt more at home in the hospital than I feel in the real world, and that is a thought that both scares me to the bone and energizes me to live. I don't ever want to be in the hospital again, but I'm okay if I need to be. I recognize that my husband, a retired peace officer, who had already buried one wife to cancer at the age of thirty-two, a husband who would never hurt a soul if he could help it, did the hardest thing he ever had to do: call 911 on his best friend.

The worst part of the coldest day in hell is that I realized what it means to be one's own worst enemy. I was trapped in a brain that was failing my body by creating hallucinations in the form of nightmares. In every nightmare I either was murdered, chose death, or caused death. I saw every death of every loved one or enemy, and they all blamed me. In my nightmares I was not always the good guy. It's a scary thing to create living daymares as a simple drug interaction between ZZZQuil,

Sertraline, edibles, and lack of sleep for three days. Add in a family history of serious mental health disorders, and I was primed for an explosion or implosion. The more I tried to sleep and the more ZZZQuil I took, the worse the daymares got. It got to the point where I was fighting my own husband, because I thought he was death here to make me pay for my sins. It didn't help that he was wearing black, and that he always showed up at the end of my nightmare. But I also hallucinated that he was someone there to save me and show me the way.

I saw Sean as my mother, my father, my brother, my sister, and at times my husband. I also saw him as my abusers, my rapists, my bullies, and my victims. There were times in my life when I was in so much pain that I lashed out verbally against anyone closest to me. On my second base I made few friends and missed two suicides. I saw their mothers blaming me for their sons' deaths. I was accepting death because it was what I thought I deserved, but I was terrified because in the end I didn't want to die. I was drowning and trying desperately to get to shore. I didn't want to kill anyone, and I was trying to stop murders I knew were coming. In reality I was running around a field, half naked, in December, screaming, "Silence!" and, "It never made any sense!" I'm so glad my mother-in-law saw how, for lack of a better word, insane I was acting. She called my husband to come home from Dallas immediately. He got to me before I took too many more pills. He did the hardest thing he could do to save me. My mother also arrived in time to see me in the hospital before I was transferred three hours away. I was still going in and out of consciousness, and none of it made any sense. I have no idea what was reality, and after my third escape attempt the poor rural hospital staff learned to lock the doors.

I thought I was Forrest Gump, running through the hospital barefoot, trying to start my year-long run. The hospital staff wouldn't let Sean back, so he sat in the waiting room and saw me escape. He would stay seated until he saw the orderlies or nurses, then point down the hall to where I went. I attempted to talk a janitor out of his shoes. And I was screaming, "Run, Forrest, run!" at the top of my lungs. In my head I made it out of the ER. I remember the cold grass and frost on my feet, and I remember deciding that I needed shoes before I went any further. The nurses or Sean would coax me back into my room, and I would lie back down to go to sleep.

I also thought I was a Russian sleeper agent here to kill JFK and make sure Oswald took the fall. But I didn't want to kill President Kennedy and chose to try to defect. Oswald knew my plan to spill Russian secrets and ratted me out. So I thought I was on the run from the KGB and needed to get to the CIA in time to defect and save a man's life. In those delusions I would quietly tiptoe away from my captors and hide until I figured out how to escape. If I was found I would yell, "Bomb!" and throw an article of clothing at them and take off running. In reality I was just yelling from a cage or running in circles inside a locked hospital waiting room. It didn't help that I was listed as an escape artist and combative with authority. It also didn't help that I was being transferred three hours in the back of a locked sheriff's vehicle. That was the longest three hours of my life, lying and crying while thinking my parents, the Russian sleeper agents who trained me, were going to kill these innocent deputies in the front seat. It certainly doesn't help that my parents gave me a Russian name in the 1980s, and that I have a Russian tattoo on my forearm.

But the best delusion of all was that I thought I was either Donald Trump on the eve of inciting a mass insurrection, or Elon Musk escaping time agents to save humanity from itself by jumpstarting interspace travel 2500 years early. I also thought the hospital bathroom was a TARDIS.

I have a theory of why some people seem to attract so many psychopaths in their life: that the brighter you let yourself shine, the darker the people become who want to tear you down. Those people saw something in me, and they wanted to destroy me. And I nearly let them. More than once. People like my grandfather or Arthur or John are so unhappy that they cannot bear the thought of anyone shining brighter than them. I'm learning never to listen to those kinds of people anymore, to lean on the good people in my life and shut out the bad.

My mental health deteriorated during the pandemic. When Vanessa Guillén disappeared in April 2020, I followed her case with a sick hope that she would be found alive. When her body was discovered, I grieved. Women around the U.S. started sharing the hashtag #iamvanessaguillen and their stories. When I shared mine, women I had been stationed with told me they had the same abusers, and I felt sick. But good has come out of her death. An awakening has happened, and people are angry. People like my friend and colleague Lisa Carrington Firmin, who has written a forthright book in which she included part of my story. Bills are being passed, and people are taking our stories more seriously. I am finally enrolled at the VA and am seeking proper counseling for what happened to me. Some veterans have visible wounds, but the invisible are now coming forward. If you take away anything from my story, I hope it will be this: No one leaves the military, or life, unscathed.

About the Author

Stesha Colby-Lynch is a Marine veteran. Before writing her own book, parts of her story appeared in *Voices of America: Veterans and Military Families Tell Their Own Stories*, edited by April Brown and Ethan Casey, and *Stories From the Front: Pain, Betrayal, and Resilience on the MST Battlefield* by Lisa Carrington Firmin.

Colby-Lynch is an avid supporter of veterans in higher education and currently serves as the Director of Veterans Services for Stephen F. Austin State University. After leaving the Marines in 2010, she used the GI Bill at Texas Christian University and has been working in higher education ever since.

She lives in Nacogdoches, Texas with her husband Sean and their pack of dogs: Greyson, Hercules, and the twins, Annie and Augie. She loves traveling with friends, hiking with her pack, paddle boarding, and anything else in the outdoors except rock climbing.

About Blue Ear Books

In 2009 journalist Ethan Casey, author of the landmark travel book *Alive and Well in Pakistan* (praised as "magnificent" by Ahmed Rashid, author of *Taliban* and *Descent into Chaos*), decided to take control of the publication and promotion of his own books, rather than remain subject to the whims and vicissitudes of a perpetually and radically changing publishing industry.

That led to the founding of Blue Ear Books, through which Casey and a small group of colleagues publish a select list of books by authors with distinctive professional and personal perspectives on the international world in the 21st century. To learn more, visit:

www.blueearbooks.com

VETERANS' STORIES FROM BLUE EAR BOOKS

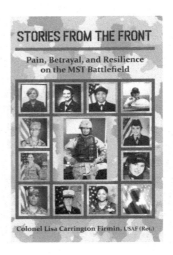
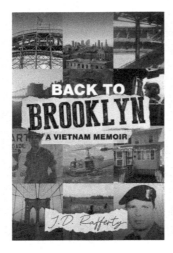

www.blueearbooks.com